Talking Texts

Innovative

recipes

for

intensive

reading

Pilgrims

Randal Holme

Longman

Longman Group UK Limited,
Longman House, Burnt Mill, Harlow,
Essex CM20 2JE, England
and Associated Companies throughout the world.

© Longman Group UK Limited 1991

This book is produced in association with Pilgrims
Language Courses Limited of Canterbury, England.

First published 1991

Set in 10/12 Cheltenham ITC Book

Produced by Longman Singapore Publishers (Pte) Ltd

Printed in Singapore

British Library Cataloguing in Publication Data
Holme, Randal
    Talking texts: innovative recipes for intensive
reading.
    (Pilgrims Longman Resource Books)
    1. Non-English speaking students. Curriculum subjects:
    English language. Teaching
    I. Title II. Series
428.2407

ISBN 0 582 07002 3

Illustrations
Cover illustrated by Pippa Sterne

ACKNOWLEDGEMENTS
We are grateful to Faber & Faber Ltd for permission to
reproduce the poem 'Originality' by Chinweizu from
Voices from Twentieth Century Africa & the poem
'Hospital Visits' from *Collected Poems* by Philip Larkin.

A letter from the Series Editors

Dear Teacher,

This series of teachers' resource books has developed from Pilgrims' involvement in running courses for learners of English and for teachers and teacher trainers.

Our aim is to pass on ideas, techniques and practical activities which we know work in the classroom. Our authors, both Pilgrims teachers and like-minded colleagues in other organisations, present accounts of innovative procedures which will broaden the range of options available to teachers working within communicative and humanistic approaches.

We would be very interested to receive your impressions of the series. If you notice any omissions that we ought to rectify in future editions, or if you think of any interesting variations, please let us know. We will be glad to acknowledge all contributions that we are able to use.

Seth Lindstromberg
Series Editor

Mario Rinvolucri
Series Consultant

Pilgrims Language Courses
Canterbury
Kent
CT1 3HG
England

Randal Holme

Randal Holme was born in London in 1948 and was educated at Westminster School and at the University of Essex. Periods of work and travel in the USA, South America and Asia were at first alternated with postgraduate studies at London, Essex and York Universities. He worked on ESL programmes for school children in both Britain and Australia. He has taught EFL and ESP and has trained teachers and written materials in Europe, the Middle East and Africa. He now works as ESP adviser to the University of Marien N'gouabi and is head of the Overseas Development Administration and British Council ELT project in the Peoples' Republic of Congo. He is married with two young children.

Contents

Index of activities

ACTIVITY	LEVEL	FOCUS
2.23 **Preteacher** Students preteach vocabulary	Elementary +	Using dictionaries, explaining the meanings of words, rapid reading
2.24 **Dictionary game 1 The word race** Students race to master unfamiliar vocabulary	Elementary +	Using dictionaries, rapid reading, discussing procedures
2.25 **Dictionary game 2 The snake pit** Using dictionaries to create an alternative text	Elementary +	Using dictionaries, reading out loud, rapid reading
2.26 **Textual bluff** A textual variation on the game *Call My Bluff*	Lower intermediate +	Deducing word meanings from context, defining words
2.27 **Cloze charades** Missing words are mimed back into the text	Elementary +	Reading comprehension, mime and constructing text
2.28 **Thinking metaphorically 1 Matching the metaphor** Text metaphors are remade	Intermediate +	Making up metaphors, matching words and metaphors, thinking about style
2.29 **Thinking metaphorically 2 Students' search** Students find and remake metaphors	Intermediate +	Making up metaphors, matching words and metaphors, thinking about style
2.30 **Thinking metaphorically 3 Metaphors looking for a meaning** Metaphors are isolated and given new meaning	Intermediate +	Finding meanings for metaphors, matching meanings and metaphors, thinking about style

3 HEADLINES AND TITLES

ACTIVITY	LEVEL	FOCUS
3.1 **Matching the headline to the story** A new version of the old title matching exercise	Intermediate +	Reading for gist, giving and listening to oral summaries, matching texts and titles
3.2 **Matching the title to the story** Students write their own headlines	Intermediate +	Reading for gist, giving and listening to oral summaries, matching texts and titles
3.3 **Headline or title expansion** Titles are expanded into texts	Lower intermediate +	Asking and answering questions, predicting a text from its title, comparing a predicted text and a real text
3.4 **True title, false title** Finding the correct title for a text	Lower intermediate +	Reading for gist, discussing the purpose of a text
3.5 **True text, false text** Distinguishing real from imagined texts	Intermediate +	Reading for gist, inventing titles, making oral summaries, asking and answering questions

Introduction

WHAT IS THIS BOOK ABOUT?

There is a slight tendency among language teachers to think that the only true route to language learning is aural, that time spent on reading and not in communicating is wasted. Yet even the most aural teachers will at some moment introduce written language into their class. The written word may be disguised in some way. It might be made to sound spontaneous like normal speech. It may be intended to be no more than the prompt that gets people talking. It could simply be the lesson notes jotted down before class. One way or another, the text creeps in.

Perhaps it is exaggerated, this idea of text getting into the communicative lesson almost by stealth. Yet if you see language learning as mastering the four very separate skills of reading, writing, speaking and understanding, with an emphasis on the last two, then perhaps it must be so. For if your priority is to encourage students to speak, then texts would disturb the communicative flow and reading them would be a waste of the class time that should be devoted to aural practice. My approach to skills is more integrative, not simply in the sense of good speaking depending on good listening, but of reading enriching speech. The object of this book is not the teaching of reading skills, rather it is to show ways to put written language into the spoken arena, to get the text into play. The aim is also to make texts more memorable, to help students to incorporate what they have learnt from the text into their language and thus to read more effectively.

Some of these activities spring from classic ELT exercises. These may act as reminders or show fresh approaches to tried and tested formulae. Some may help teachers to think more critically about their own approaches. None of them are intended to be rigid prescriptions, instead they are all ways to stimulate your own classroom creativity. You may even want to rewrite the book as a set of further variations.

This goal of flexibility has made it impossible to estimate the time that a given activity will take. In this, much will depend on the teaching style and the student response. Also, the length of time needed for a text centred activity depends upon the nature of the text and on the ability of the students to cope with it.

WHAT IS A TEXT?

Perhaps 'text' is too vague a term. It could be anything written, from a one-word poem to a seven-volume treatise on cosmology.

For our purposes here, a text is a written piece of language which is short enough to be dealt with in the context of one or two lessons. It may be one of a series, or it could be an extract from a longer work which is being studied in its entirety. In that case, this book will provide ideas on how to treat different parts of a work in a variety of ways and so could stimulate student interest in an extended study.

The sample texts

I have, for certain activities, provided sample texts to illustrate the procedure to be followed. You may, if you wish, use these sample texts with your students. However, don't forget that they are included only by way of example. The activities are designed to work with any text which fits the general requirements of that activity.

Where an activity requires a particular type of text (such as poetry, dialogue or a newspaper article), I have noted this under the heading 'suggested text'. If the activity can be used with any type of text, I have specified this under the 'materials' heading in the margin. A text often supposes something authentic and this may be why many of these activities are aimed at the upper intermediate or advanced bands. However, purpose-written texts are also covered and quite a few of the activities work at the elementary level.

English for Special or Academic Purposes

I have particularly tried to include activities for ESP and EAP teachers since much of what they do involves text work. Accordingly, many of the activities here apply to literary and technical texts in a straightforward way. This can be true even where the sample text I give is for a lower-level general English class. There are two main reasons why the sample texts in this book tend not to be ESP and EAP texts. Firstly, good lower-level general English texts are relatively scarce. Secondly, any particular ESP or EAP text would be directly useful to a relatively small proportion of teachers. That is, for example, a text on the specifications of oral anaesthetics might well not be usable with anyone but (would-be) dentists.

WHY USE TEXTS AT ALL?

The idea of this book is not to see text-work as a disagreeable necessity but rather to insist upon it as making a positive and exciting contribution to the language learning process.

Many language teachers spend a lot of their class time working with texts. A text may be introduced into the class for one or more of the following reasons:

1 It is thought that it will form a useful basis for a lesson and provide good language input.
2 It is to be used in conjunction with other texts to improve reading skills.

3 It is held to be valuable or worthy of study in itself.

4 It is seen as motivating because it is an example of the kind of material to which students may be given access by the language they are learning.

5 It is requested by the class.

6 It is prescribed by or found relevant to another course over whose content the teacher has no control (the ESP reason).

7 It is prescribed by a syllabus over which the teacher has no control.

Any combination of these reasons may force texts upon students or upon teachers. Yet even the most negative of them does not preclude an approach which, instead of letting the words stare coldly at the student, takes them off the page and into the class. Even if texts are not immediately captivating, they can still be a frame for something more interesting, something more suited to the students' mood and inclination on the day they are studied. A text can make a lesson and a lesson can remake a text.

READING, READING OUT LOUD AND LEARNER AUTONOMY

It should now be clear that the idea here is not to write another book about reading. Any activity based on written language presupposes reading of some kind if only by the teacher to the class. All of these activities engage students in intensive reading, for gist, for close understanding or for both. Their combined effect may be to improve reading speed and efficiency but this is not the overall aim. The purpose, rather, is that reading should enrich speaking, writing and understanding.

Some of the activities involve reading out loud. This technique has fallen out of favour with some teachers because it is thought to encourage subvocalisation and so impede the raising of reading speed. A behaviourist might regard reading out loud as a way to instill bad pronunciation since students might be tempted to apply pronunciation forms from their own language to the target language so, for example, the French student of English would pronounce certain letter combinations in a French way. Both of these arguments rest on assumptions about the learner that I do not share. They assume that the learner is the passive victim of the method and has neither intellect nor autonomy enough to learn from mistakes or to think critically about the limitations of a given lesson. My view of the learner is of someone able to adapt their strategies to circumstances and get the most from different approaches. The learner of this book does not sit compounding errors like a caged bird, but rather is capable of taking an active role in the learning process.

On the basis of the same assumption, some of the activities insist that the students must themselves decide on their own approach to a task. They must negotiate procedures. Useful language is thereby generated and the group formation central to language learning is advanced. Other activities may provide the language with which to discuss a certain facet of a text. Two kinds of language are thus put into play. The student becomes more familiar with the language we use to talk *about* the text and with the language *in* the text itself.

FINDING TEXTS

The trick in finding good texts is to see almost every kind of publication or even unpublished work as a potential source of good learning material. What you select and how you use it must ultimately depend on you, your students and their learning goals. Teaching situations are ever-changing and what may not seem useful one year could be so the next. It is useful to cut out and keep what ever strikes you as having potential even if the level or subject matter does not suit the class of the moment.

Text banks are useful both for teachers and schools – with classification according to title, subject matter, level and suitability for certain activities.

Finally, if all normal sources fail to give you what you want, then you can always try writing texts yourself. Not only can you make the language level and subject matter of the text exactly fit your requirements, but you may even be surprised to find that it is better than anything else available!

Randal Holme
Brazzaville
Spring 1990

CHAPTER 1

Print into pictures, pictures into print

People respond visually to different degrees but for everyone under-standing may often mean making mental pictures of some kind. Even abstract words are often 'seen'. *Heat* could suggest a bright red haze, *solitude* the person on an empty beach. Teachers exploit this tendency when they use pictures to involve students in a text or get them to draw in order to help them express their understanding of what they read.

When asked to draw, some students will complain that they cannot. Perhaps teachers will sympathise when they look at their own clumsy efforts on the blackboard. But this should not be a problem. Incompe-tent drawing can often enhance communication. It gives meaning to such a basic but often empty question as 'What's that?' It forces students to explain and so helps them to remember. Incompetent drawing is a kind of information gap. Competent drawing motivates discussion and assists memory. So, with drawing you win either way. Picture making can even be purely imaginative so that neither student nor teacher ever puts pen to paper.

The content of a text can also be shown as a diagram or flow chart. The student can thus map a written argument and make clear what is most important. The flow chart is particularly popular with ESP teachers, perhaps because it is so often used to clarify technical processes or to discover the logic of a procedure. It can provide the prompts that help the students recall text to each other and the pattern that may make it more memorable. Other types of diagram, such as graphs or maps, can achieve a similar end or emphasise different parts of the text.

Pictures and diagrams can also provide a way into text. They can create interest in what the text may be about. They can provide a visual context for texts whose subject matter is not immediately accessible, perhaps because they are about a remote place or time. Readers often pick up magazines and scan the pictures, pause over one that interests them then search for the explanation of what it is or why it is there. The picture thus makes the reading purposeful. Even in one's own language, dense text can be a daunting prospect, in a foreign language it is doubly so. A pictorial introduction can make that prospect an easier one. It can map the student's reading matter and show a path through its complex-ity.

1.1

LEVEL
Elementary+

FOCUS
Brainstorming, character description, imagining scenarios, talking about the past

MATERIALS
Class set of a biography, a picture of the subject

PICTURE BIOGRAPHIES

This activity is helpful as an introduction to the work or life of a person who is being studied in a course but it can also successfully stand alone.

SUGGESTED TEXT
Short biography or autobiography plus a photograph or painting of the person in question. The picture should reveal the character of its subject. Biographies or autobiographies can be edited downwards in level, for use with lower intermediate or elementary students.

Preparation

1 Think how the life in question divides into different themes. For most lives the titles of the themes might be something like: 'Birth, childhood and family'; 'Education'; 'Working life'; 'Loves'; 'Children'; 'Death'; though, of course, not all of these may be relevant. Write the themes on the board according to the biography in question.

Procedure

1 Distribute or display copies of the picture so that every student can see it. Give no information about the subject of the picture. (Some students may recognise it, others may not.)

2 Brainstorm adjectives to describe the person in the picture. Write the adjectives on the board as students suggest them and insert your own additions for vocabulary expansion but along the lines suggested by the students. Character adjectives should not reflect your own view of the subject.

3 Put the students into as many groups as there are themes. Give each group a theme. So, for example, there would be a Birth, childhood and family group and a Working life group, etc.

4 Ask each group to invent a scenario appropriate both to their theme and to the kind of life they would expect the person in the picture to lead.

5 Explain that a scenario should be a situation with no conclusion. A simple example under Family might be: 'He is eighteen and his father refuses to let him study what he wants', or under Love: 'The woman he is in love with tells him she wants to marry someone else', or under Death: 'At a relatively young age he learns that he has a fatal disease'. Some groups might think that more complex or stranger scenarios are appropriate, others may have recognised the subject and will suggest scenarios that actually come from his or her life. Stress to the students that it is important they do not recount how the scenario actually unfolds at this stage.

6 Ask each group to present their scenario to the class, beginning with birth and ending with death.

7 As the scenarios are presented, the class should discuss how the character would behave, what they would do and feel. The class should keep the character of the person, as decided by their

brainstormed adjectives, strongly in mind so that if they have been judged passionate then their character should respond passionately. The discussion might run as follows:

Student 1   His lover says she wants to marry someone else. (The scenario)
Student 2   He shoots himself. (A suggested response)
Student 3   No, he pretends he's going to shoot himself.
Student 4   That's right and his lover cries 'Don't!'.
Student 5   No, she just says 'Go on, do it then and stop wasting time'.

8 When each group has presented their scenario, distribute the biography.
9 Ask the class to read the biography and to decide if it is consistent with the kind of person they have collectively portrayed. Try to put the picture in the context of the biography by asking students questions such as: 'What had just happened when it was taken/painted?', 'Where had the subject reached in their life?' etc.

EXTENSION

10 In small groups the class rewrite the real biography so that it follows the life which they invented for the person. They should do this while trying to change the original text as little as possible.

VARIATION 1

You produce the text.

1 You write a short biography of a friend or colleague of yours and show the class their picture.
2 Proceed as in the original exercise.

VARIATION 2

Write your own biography.

1 Ask the students to invent the scenarios for your life then discuss how you would react.
2 Give them your text. Not surprisingly, many students are very interested in the lives of their teachers!

VARIATION 3

Use biographies of the lives of composers. These can often be found in the notes that come with records, CDs or cassettes. Use a piece of music by the composer instead of a picture.

1 Brainstorm adjectives that describe character and write them on the board. These should be general, not specific to a particular person. Guide the brainstorm so that many different character types are included.
2 Play your piece of music. If the piece is long you may prefer to play several contrasting extracts.
3 Students listen and describe the character of the composer as it is conveyed by the music. They do this by writing down adjectives from the selection on the board that they think are appropriate.
4 Proceed as from step 3 of the original exercise.

VARIATION 4

For extended biographies and longer reading or research assignments.

1 At step 9 of the original version, students write down all the scenarios and their reactions to them.

2 Students go away from the class to read the same biography or to research the life in question. Students edit their scenarios in order to make them fit the real life.

3 Form groups and assign each group an edited scenario. The groups act out their scenario after first practising it. They can either write a script or improvise.

ACKNOWLEDGEMENT

The idea of the scenario comes to me from *Strategic Interaction: Learning Languages through Scenarios* (De Pietro 1988).

1.2

LEVEL
Upper
intermediate+

FOCUS
Describing
character,
describing and
generalising about
styles of writing

MATERIALS
Class sets of
literary texts by
different writers,
pictures of the
writers, Blu-tack or
sellotape

WHAT WOULD THEY WRITE?

This activity complements Activity 1.1, *Picture biographies* but can also stand alone. It gets at texts through the character of their writer, but it concentrates on the writer's work rather than their life story. It helps students to talk about style and match ways of writing to types of character.

You will deal here with several writers and several styles but among them there may be one you are planning to concentrate on later. This kind of contrastive exercise can help to stress the uniqueness of a particular kind of writing and so help to stimulate an interest in it.

SUGGESTED TEXTS AND PICTURES

A selection of three or more literary texts by different writers and pictures of the writers. A class set of each text and enough pictures for them to be easily seen by all of the students.

Procedure

1 Divide the class into as many groups as you have writers and ask each group to appoint a secretary. Give each group a picture.

2 Brainstorm character adjectives that fit the subjects of the picture.

3 The secretaries should write down the words that emerge from the brainstorm. Slot in suggestions as you circulate from group to group.

4 The students speculate on the kind of works the writers in the pictures would write. They relate their speculations to the character in the picture. It does not matter if students recognise a writer as they can merely say what they know about that writer and relate it or not to their idea of the character.

5 Ask each group to discuss their conclusions with the rest of the class.

6 Take the pictures of the writers and stick them on the board or wall with Blu-tack or sellotape.

7 Distribute the texts to the students and time their reading at about three times your own speed.

8 When they have finished reading, ask them to 'attribute' the text by writing its title or first line under the appropriate writer's picture. Different students may attribute texts differently.

9 Ask students why they attributed texts in the way they did. If they disagree, encourage a class discussion.

10 Tell the students who really wrote which text.

EXTENSION

1 Select a student to role play each writer.

2 Ask the class to question the 'writers' about why they wrote what they did. The writers should try to justify themselves in terms of the kind of person that the class has decided they are.

WHAT WOULD THEY PAINT?

This is almost the reverse of Activity 1.2 *What would they write?* As such, it is less about a pictorial introduction to a text than about a visual response to one.

SUGGESTED TEXT

A short biography of a painter, divided into sections, each representing a distinct part of the painter's life. Enough copies for each student to have one section each. Good results can be obtained by writing a spoof.

Procedure

1 Give out one part of the divided text to each student and ask them to read it. Each part can be assigned several times over if you have a large class or some pieces can be left unassigned if you have a very small one.

2 Ask each student to read their part of the biography, then to imagine a painting that reflects the kind of life or work that one part describes. Ask them to:

• Think broadly about the subject and style of the painting.

• Think broadly about the composition then about the detail – they can make notes or draw a picture diagram showing what is where. Their ideas must relate strongly to their part of the passage. For example, if a 'blue period' is described then the painting should illustrate this.

1.3

LEVEL
Upper
intermediate+

FOCUS
Describing an
imaginary picture,
role playing

MATERIALS
Class set of a
biography of a
painter, divided
into sections

3 After each student has composed a picture, draw as many empty rectangles on the board as you have students.

4 Ask the student with the first part of the passage to go to the board and to explain the first rectangle as if it were their imaginary picture. They should not draw inside the frame but should merely write a title underneath. It is best to start with a confident student or with your own example in order to avoid a sticky beginning.

5 Repeat with the other rectangles, thus building up an imaginary chronological exhibition of the artist's work.

6 Ask the students to role play visitors to the gallery where their paintings are displayed. They take the entire text as a catalogue and use it to talk informatively to each other about the pictures.

1.4

LEVEL
Intermediate+

FOCUS
Writing and discussing impressions of a picture, relating a picture to a text

MATERIALS
Class set of a literary extract, a related picture

EVOCATIVE PICTURES

Like many teachers you may already introduce texts with pictures in order to emphasise something important or to give the right atmosphere or setting. Perhaps sometimes you're left with the feeling that the relationship of the picture and text has neither been fully exposed or exploited. The impact of the picture is lost as the meaning of the text is puzzled out. This exercise locks picture and text together. It makes the relationship between picture and text into a reading objective. The nature of the relationship is the puzzle that must be solved.

SUGGESTED TEXT AND PICTURE

A text which has an emotional impact, such as a literary extract or poem. A picture which you find in some way evocative of the atmosphere or subject matter of the text. The text and picture do not have to be directly about each other. The picture is best shown in slide form, though a print or plate for circulation round the class can work very well.

Procedure

1 Quickly circulate or flash the picture, allowing each student only a few seconds to look at it.

2 Tell the class that they have one minute to write down any thoughts they have about the picture. They may write in note form or in formal sentences.

3 Ask a student to read out what they have written then ask them to justify it. Invite the class to ask questions. Ask them to discuss their different ideas. If the discussion flags, repeat with another student.

4 Distribute the text and ask the students to discover why you have matched it with the picture.

5 Show the picture again. Let the class see it for as long as they want.

6 Encourage discussion by asking such questions as:
- Does the text tell you anything about the picture, directly or indirectly?
- Does the picture tell you anything about the text?
- Do the writer and the artist see their subjects differently?
- Does the picture change the way you think about the text?

If no one wants to answer this kind of question, do not worry, just pause, then answer it yourself quietly but in a provocative way. You could even say the opposite of what really seems true, just to get a response.

If there is a student who is not contributing, ask them to sum up what someone else has just said. Imply you have not understood and need the help of a quieter, more rational person.

VARIATION
Use a short passage of music instead of a picture. Play the music at Steps 1 and 5.

MATCHING RESPONSES

This activity uses a picture to interpret a text and the text to interpret a picture. It encourages students to describe imagined pictures and to recount imagined texts.

SUGGESTED TEXT AND PICTURE
A text which has an emotional impact, such as a literary extract or poem. A picture which you find evokes the atmosphere of a text or depicts its subject matter. The text and picture do not have to be directly about each other. Advertisements with a fairly extensive text work well.

Procedure

1 Divide the class into two groups. Give the text to Group 1 and ask them to read it and to think how they would illustrate it with one picture. The picture should not necessarily represent the text in a direct way, though at the elementary level this may be all that is possible. Get the students to construct the picture in detail. Discourage them from actually drawing as this may limit their imagination. If the students' level is high enough, suggest they think about the style of the picture and the kind of impact that it makes. Different students may suggest different pictures. The group should try to integrate them all into a single composition.

1.5

LEVEL
Elementary+

FOCUS
Expressing and discussing responses to a text, describing and discussing feelings

MATERIALS
Class set of a literary extract, a related picture

2 Show the picture to Group 2 and ask them to imagine a text that would fit the picture. They can do this in the same way as the picture group. Their ideas for the text may also run ahead of their language. This should be encouraged by preventing them from actually re-counting their text in detail. They could think first of generalities. They should ask themselves:
- Is it poetry or prose?
- Tragic or comic?
- Does it teach them or entertain them, or do both at the same time? They should not think 'what happens?' so much as 'who, or what is it about?' Only at the end get them to move from the generalities to the detail.

3 If one group finishes before the other they can write notes about their pictures or text.

4 The two groups describe their invented texts and pictures to each other.

5 The two groups exchange texts and pictures. They discuss differences between what they imagined and what they were given. Discussion can be focused by asking each group to produce five sentences and no more, showing the key differences.

1.6

LEVEL
Beginner +

FOCUS
Describing
pictures

MATERIALS
Short comic strip, a
video camera
(optional)

COMIC SCRIPT

The comic strip provides the perfect example of an interaction between text and picture. The format is already well-known to teachers and figures in many elementary text books.

Popular methods with comic strips are generally variations upon one of the following:

METHOD 1
1 White out the speech bubbles.
2 Students improvise an appropriate dialogue and write it back into the bubbles.

METHOD 2
1 White out the speech bubbles.
2 Write a short text telling the story of the comic strip.
3 Cut up the pictures and shuffle them.
4 Students arrange the pictures in order by reading your short text.

METHOD 3

1 White out the speech bubbles and present them in script form on a separate piece of paper.

2 Students decide which piece of speech belongs to which picture.

The following exercise is really an elaboration of the last two methods.

SUGGESTED TEXT

Any comic strip or extract from a comic book story. Tintin works well with intermediate and above. Many of the best comics are foreign. Teachers should not be afraid of translations since these are also authentic texts when done by a native speaker for a native speaker market.

Preparation

1 Write the speech from the comic strip on a separate piece of paper, making clear which character is speaking when. Make one copy for each student.

2 White out all the speech bubbles on the comic strip and make one copy of this version for each student.

Procedure

1 Ask the students to form small groups. Each group should have as many students as there are characters in the comic strip, plus one director.

2 Give the director in each group a copy of the comic strip with the blanked-out speech. Give the others a copy of your script. Throughout the exercise only the director should see the pictures and only the others should see the script.

3 Tell each group to imagine that they are going to make a film sequence based on the script you have given them. The directors will assign the parts then rehearse the actors and tell them what to do. The directors will use their comic pictures as if they were production notes. They will try to get the actors to follow them frame by frame and will improvise scenery and props from classroom furniture. They will try to get the dialogue to fit each frame by listening to the actors reading the script. They should describe how the characters look and try to get students to mimic their expressions and postures.

4 Allow rehearsal time according to the length of the script and the interest of the students in the activity, then get each group to perform for the rest of the class.

5 Distribute a complete version of the comic strip for reading and discussion.

EXTENSION

Get the directors to actually film a second performance if you have a video camera available. The act of filming will itself generate a lot of additional language.

VARIATION

You can also do this exercise with the comic strip illustrations to instructions, process or procedure descriptions that are found in many ESP textbooks. However, you may have to write your own script and assign roles to objects. For example, for a sequence on how to unscrew a nut you might use a script like this:

Nut	Oh no, him again. Why can't he leave me alone?
Spanner	This looks like an awkward customer, all rusted up.
Man	It won't budge!
Nut	Oh, you're hurting me!
Spanner	No strength, this chap.

The production stage can be hilarious!

1.7

LEVEL
Elementary+

FOCUS
Sentence
formation and
cohesion,
collective
paragraph writing,
reading
comprehension

MATERIALS
Class set of texts
and diagrams or
pictures

TEXTS THROUGH DIAGRAMS AND DIAGRAMS THROUGH TEXTS

This is an activity which uses diagrams, graphs, charts, maps or drawings to involve students in the subject matter of a text and to deal with its crucial vocabulary in order to make it more accessible. The activity motivates class reading by giving it an objective. The students first have the sense of fumbling for the text then the reading reveals all. The technique can work well with ESP classes.

SUGGESTED TEXT AND MATERIALS

Any text that introduces or explains a diagram. Texts with a picture that reveals their basic subject matter. Teachers who have a text and no picture or diagram can draw their own.

Preparation

1 Make a list of words or phrases that you consider crucial to the subject matter of the text in question. Write each word on a little card or slip of paper. These will be called 'key words'. The key words are underlined in the example for elementary students on page 11.

Procedure

1 If there are more students than key words, then divide the class into groups. No group should have more members than there are key words.
2 Deal out the key words to the students. If you have more than one group, each group should have a complete set of key words.
3 Check that the students understand their key words.

The Pecking Order

She did it once; she did it twice; then her parents didn't pay attention. She did it when they were walking across the wide fields on hot summer days. She did it when they were walking down the small road that went to their house.

'Come on, Marianne,' she said, 'hurry up. I want my tea. Be quick now.' Or, when she was tired, she got very angry: 'Wait, Marianne, wait, please, don't hurry. I'm not as big as you, I can't walk as fast as you can.'

The first time, her parents thought she was talking to somebody. Then they saw that there was nobody there. So it continued.

'Come on, Marianne,' they heard their daughter say one evening when they were coming home late.

When they heard another child, they were very surprised.

'Come on Juliet,' the child said, 'we're late.' They looked and saw nobody there. They decided they were imagining things.

About a week later, they were passing the same place in the road when they heard the other voice again.

'Quick now Juliet,' it said. There was nobody there and they were even more surprised when they heard a less polite voice behind Juliet.

'Get a bloody move on,' the voice said.

Then they understood. Perhaps none of them were quite there and they were walking across the countryside with a line of grumbling ghosts behind.

4 Give out copies of the diagram or picture. Students use their original key word to write a sentence about the visual.

5 Tell the student with the key word that appears first in the text to come to the board and write their sentence. The rest of the group corrects it if necessary. Whoever has the next key word comes up and writes their sentence and so on. When no student can offer a coherent follow-on, other members of their group can adjust or rewrite the sentences to make them fit. The result should be a fairly coherent paragraph.

6 When each group has produced a paragraph, hand out copies of the text and ask students to read it in order to find out how well their paragraph on the board interprets the visual.

1.8

LEVEL
Elementary+

FOCUS
Reading for gist and detail, describing a diagram, reading out loud, negotiating procedures

MATERIALS
Class set of texts and diagrams or pictures

LABELLING GAME

Texts and pictures can interact to illustrate each other. Diagrams inform about texts and texts about diagrams. ESP teachers, particularly, are fond of asking students to read a text then use the information in it to label a diagram. The labelled diagram then makes the text more informative. The activity is not only useful for ESP, it can also be an elementary reading exercise for such general language topics as 'directions'.

SUGGESTED TEXT AND PICTURE
One or two texts that explain a diagram or picture. The text should identify the features in the diagram. Technical or scientific texts are particularly good. Teachers can also prepare their own nonsense texts and 'Heath Robinson/Rube Goldberg' diagrams. This type of text will also provide good practice of the alphabet since most of the names will need spelling out. A teacher interested in this aspect should insist on correctly spelt labels. See page 13 for an example for intermediate students.

Preparation

1 Separate the diagram and text and make as many copies of both as there are students. Make sure that the labels on the diagram are removed, although it may be necessary to label one part of the diagram in order to provide the students with a starting point.

The Cup Maker

'Now this machine,' said the Manager, 'is our Chocolate-Cup Maker. Elegant, don't you think? On the right you have the mixer tank. It's that cylindrical object right under the examining light. The autospoon dips into the boiler vat, lifts liquid chocolate into the aforementioned mixer tank where the vibra blades whip it towards confectionery perfection. Then the liquid is squeezed through the snot nozzle into the cup mould where it becomes hard. The chocolate cup is then ejected from the mould by the special spring base and flies elegantly towards the cream bath. Here it is electro creamed, the cream adhering to the chocolate as a result of an electrocreamatic process. The cream cup is finally lifted on to the drying tray by my unique sympathetic levitator. Now, on to the next part of the factory.'

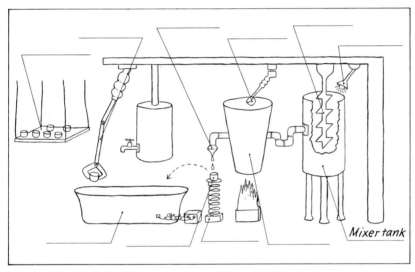

Mixer tank

© Longman Group UK Ltd 1991

Procedure

1 Divide the class into pairs.
2 Give one student in the pair a text and the other a diagram.
3 Tell the partners they cannot look at each other's papers.
4 The pairs race each other to produce the first correctly labelled diagram. The partner with the text reads it to the other, who listens and labels the diagram. If necessary they can stop, discuss the possible meanings of the text or ask each other questions.
5 Let everyone finish. Then ask them to circulate and compare their diagrams.
6 Ask one student to come to the front of the class to role play a teacher explaining the diagram. They ask the class questions and the class questions them.

1.9

LEVEL
Elementary –
intermediate

FOCUS
Discussing the
main points in a
text, reading out
loud, describing a
picture

MATERIALS
Class set of texts
and diagrams or
pictures

PICTURE CORRECTIONS

The interaction of text and picture can be used in correction exercises. The text is then set up as a series of prompts for an elaborate correction drill.

SUGGESTED TEXT AND PICTURE

One or two texts that explain a diagram or picture. The text should identify the features in the picture or the diagram. Technical or scientific texts are particularly good. This is also useful for such popular ESP activities as describing an office or describing the plan of a building. Many commercial English courses contain pictures of offices with texts for practising location and office vocabulary.

Preparation

1 Separate the picture and text and make as many copies of both as there are students.

2 Change the text so that it represents things slightly differently from the picture as in this example written for elementary students:

> I live near Rainwall. It is a village of five houses and a post office. We own the farm called Great Coumbe. Great Coumbe is just a farm house and a barn. The Dour Mountains lie to the East. The River Holt flows straight through the middle of the village then passes to the North of our house. Beyond the Dour mountains lie the Griffon Pines. These woods extend all the way to the Windless Lake. A railway line passes to the South of our village. There is a little station called Coumbe Halt. It's something of a joke around here. We call it 'The Halt where they never do.' That's our modern railway for you.

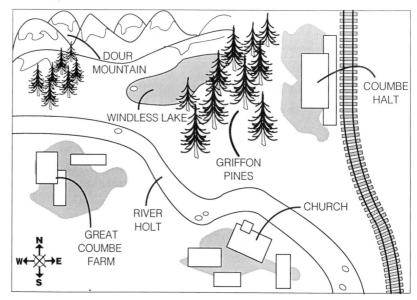

© Longman Group UK Ltd 1991

Procedure

1 Divide the class into pairs. Give one partner the picture and the other the text.
2 Tell the partners that they cannot look at each other's papers.
3 Say that there are errors in the text which must be corrected in the following way and within a stated, limited time. The partner with the text reads it aloud to the one with the picture and the partner with the picture corrects statements when they do not match the information in the picture. For this example, the discussion might follow these lines:

Student 1   It's a village of five houses and a post office.
Student 2   No, it's not, it's got three houses and a church.

The student with the text then corrects the text.

4 Ask students with the text to form pairs and those with the pictures to also form pairs.
5 The text pairs compare their corrections and the picture pairs devise a few questions about the picture to check that the text is now correct.
6 The class works together. Picture students put their questions to the text students. Any remaining problems are sorted out.

VARIATION 1

The text is correct and the picture is wrong. The text students write the questions and the picture students answer them.

VARIATION 2

This is a maddening variation that not only provides practice in the areas outlined but will also get students involved in often furious argument. An excellent way to needle precise-minded students!

1 Give half the class the text and half the class the picture. Do not say that the text and picture are different. Tell the text students that they will have a limited time for reading. They may take notes about things they think are important. While they are reading, get the picture students to write a short description of the picture. When the time is up, take back the texts and pictures. Text students can keep their notes and picture students their descriptions.
2 Put the students in pairs and tell them that they are going to be examined on their knowledge of both text and picture after a given period of time. Make it clear that they will be involved in an information exchange and that they cannot look at each other's papers. Between them they must find out as much as possible about both picture and text.
3 If students become deadlocked or furious with each other, tell them what you have done, give out the texts again and proceed as from Step 3 of the original exercise.

VARIATION 3
Use a flow chart instead of a picture. This will allow you to give the same treatment to more complex texts, particularly those describing procedures and processes. For a fuller description of flow charts see the flow chart activities in this chapter.

1.10

LEVEL
Elementary –
upper intermediate

FOCUS
Plotting a path
through a text,
recounting a text
from a diagram

MATERIALS
Class set of any
text

TEXTUAL TREASURE MAP

Think of the text as a verbal landscape through which you and your students have to go in search of its meaning. You do not know which way to go but you have your clues and the text itself to guide you. This activity introduces the idea of the flow chart or critical path.

The Great Bell of Harken
The great bell of Harken was our bell. It was silver and all men wanted to hear it. People sat at the cafe in the old square and waited for it to ring. At night you could see the moon and stars in it. That's why people said that Harken had two moons and two skies.

Every morning at six, Tom Burlington went to ring it. He walked into the stone tower and pulled the big rope. He was a strong man but the bell never made a sound. He used to sing 'BOOM BOOM' and some said that the bell rang him.

'Can't you hear it?' Tom cried.

'Not a sound', we used to tell him.

'There's only two times you'll hear that bell,' he laughed. 'One time's at the beginning and the other time's at the end.'

'The end of what?' I asked him and he just laughed at my stupidity.

'And what really are you waiting for?' I asked all those patient people in the cafe.

'The bell,' they said, 'the bell.' All of them sat like school children at their desks and the waiter poured out another lesson.

Clues
1 The question that made Tom laugh
2 Harken's second moon
3 What the bell never did
4 The man who was in the tower
5 The second time you hear it
6 What people waited for in the cafe
7 What all men wanted to hear
8 The first time you hear it
9 Who the people in the cafe are like

© Longman Group UK Ltd 1991

Preparation

1 Imagine you are going to write comprehension questions on the most important points in the text. Decide what these points will be then write your questions in the form of simple riddles or clues. These could often be just sentences or phrases lifted whole from the text. For example, for the text on page 16, one such clue could be: 'It's silver and men love the sound' (The Great Bell of Harken). The solutions to these clues will then be the words that remind you of the most important ideas in the text.
2 Draw a 'text map' under the clues. The map should consist of as many circles as you have clues. Number the circles in random order, as in the example below.

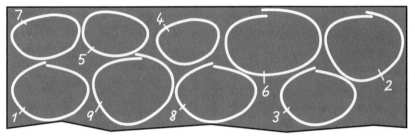

Procedure

1 Hand each student a copy of the text and a copy of the map and clues.
2 Tell the students that each circle on the map represents a place. If the circle is numbered 2 then the students look at clue 2. The answer to the clue gives the name of the place. They should write the name on the circle. For the example text and map they should get the following:

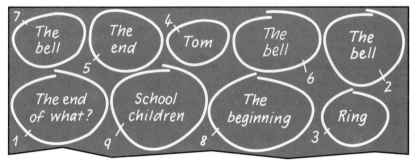

3 Tell the students to work alone, read the text and label all the circles.
4 When a student has finished, take the text away from them and ask them to draw a route that takes them through all the places and which ends at the point they think most important to them. The route is an interpretation and does not have to follow the order of the text exactly but it should make sense in textual terms. If the text has an argument, then the route should make that clear. Students may have

to explain why they took the route that they did and why they chose their particular destination.

5 Ask one student to draw the circles on the board.

6 Ask the rest of the class to dictate the names of the circles.

7 Ask the class to agree on a route and to dictate it to the student at the board. They must justify their itinerary. If there is disagreement over which way to go, the class should argue over the alternatives. If each case seems equally good then the map can show different routes and the class will divide into rival groups of textual wanderers. Simple texts will probably show one route.

VARIATION

For students who have already done the first activity.

1 Divide the text in two or find two texts.

2 Divide the class into two groups and give each a different text. Each group prepare clues and a map for the other.

3 Proceed as from Step 1 of the original activity.

1.11

LEVEL
Elementary+

FOCUS
Reading for gist, expressing understanding of a text

MATERIALS
Class set of a text

THE TEXTUAL TREE, AN ORGANIC FLOW CHART

All texts have an argument of some kind. This is not to say that they are all obvious expressions of opinion but that they move from one point to another and attempt to carry their reader with them. Sometimes the argument is not logical but metaphorical, shifting through an association of things, yet it is always there in anything readable, showing a development of some kind. This activity asks students to chart and discuss that development. The idea of representing a text in terms other than itself, as a tree in this case, may seem strange to some, but this shift into a more metaphorical thought pattern can be liberating.

SUGGESTED TEXT

Any showing the development of a central idea. The development could be narrative, showing the consequences of a central event or events. Equally it could be procedural, technical, scientific, polemical or descriptive.

Preparation

Think of your text as having some important point of departure, an event or idea that will determine the development of all others. Decide what this is.

Procedure

1 Hand out the texts and give students a very short time to skim through and to grasp as much of the argument as they can.

2 Take back the texts.

3 Tell students to imagine that they are representing that text as a tree without leaves. The tree might be squat and straggling or tall and neatly pruned. The shape of their tree should represent their first impression of the text.

4 The students draw their tree.

5 Hand back the texts and give the students a longer period to read it and understand it thoroughly. Sort out any comprehension problems.

6 Ask the students to make their trees express the text more closely. They should think of the most important or basic idea in the text and name the trunk after it. They should see that trunk as growing out and finally flowering into other ideas and should label the branches accordingly. The following text for advanced students might give the tree below.

Winstanley thought that from half to two thirds of England was not properly cultivated. One third of England was a barren waste, which Lords of the Manor would not permit the poor to cultivate. If the waste land of England were manured by her children, it would become in a few years the richest, the strongest and most flourishing land in the world. The price of corn would fall. An increase in the cultivated area, the Digger Poet Robert Coster added, would bring down the price of land and therewith the cost of living. Common land cultivation could allow for capital investment in improve-ments without sacrificing the interests of commoners. There was land enough to maintain ten times the present population, abolish begging and crime and make England 'first of nations.'

Christopher Hill, *The World Turned Upside Down*, Peregrine 1988 p 128

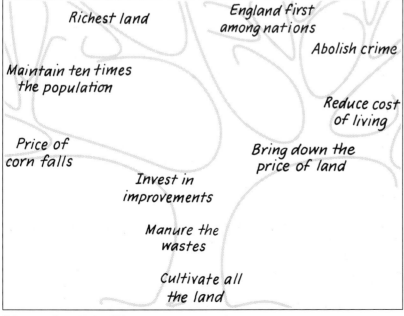

© Longman Group UK Ltd 1991

7 Students compare their labelled trees.

8 Draw a tree on the board. Ask the students to help you label it. They should use their own trees as a reference point and discuss alternatives, finally reaching a class concensus.

1.12

LEVEL
Elementary+

FOCUS
Drawing flow charts, discussing the argument of a text

MATERIALS
Class set of a text

WAYS WITH FLOW CHARTS 1

Flow charts are a way to map the sequence of procedures and processes with which we make even the most simple things happen. At a high level, the discovery of the sequence of thought which an experienced doctor uses to make a diagnosis can help the computer programmer to design a program to help less experienced peers. At a low level, the flow chart could simply clarify the steps involved in frying an egg. So the following passage could be expressed in the flow chart below.

Frying an egg? Yes, well, first I've got to get one, haven't I. Sounds obvious but there you are. I get it out of the fridge and break it, no, well, first I have to put some oil in a pan and heat the oil up, then after I break the egg into the pan, then you, well, it depends how you want the egg doesn't it, sunnyside up or down. If it's down you have to turn it over, if it's up then you just cook it on the one side. Either way it ends up getting put on a plate and eaten.

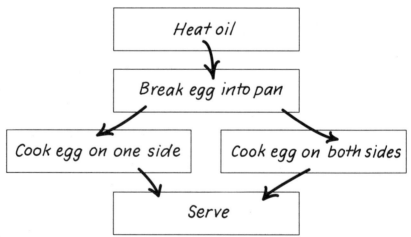

The text here is lower intermediate but the flow chart is elementary. A flow chart exercise can thus help a lower level student to discover the argument of a difficult text. Even native speakers use flow charts in this way. ESP teachers in particular may not just be involved in teaching language but in orientating students towards the demands of a new type of subject matter. For some students, the idea of a logical progression is itself alien. For such students the flow chart exercise is educative in the broadest sense.

The ESP teacher will often be dealing with texts that describe procedures and processes, though generally in a more logical way than the one above. Yet flow chart exercises are by no means the preserve of the ESP class. Flow charts can express a student's understanding of narratives and dilemmas as well. At their most complicated they can process the plots and arguments of entire books.

SUGGESTED TEXT

Any describing processes, procedures or dilemmas. Texts with narrative progression or argument.

Preparation

1 Draw a flow chart of your text.
2 White out the words in the boxes and make one copy of the blank chart for each student.

Procedure

1 Put the students into pairs. Give each pair two copies of the text and one blank chart.
2 Explain the idea of the chart to the students. It may be useful to illustrate the concept of flow charts using the egg example on page 20.
3 Each pair fills in one flow chart from the text. While they are working, draw a blank chart on the board.
4 When they have finished, tell the class that they must standardise their charts. They circulate and show their charts to each other and change them in an attempt to get the same chart. Small differences in the wording of the labels are allowed but not differences in content. If there are differences, students should argue their case. Finally, the minority must bow to the wishes of the majority. If no consensus emerges, you decide on one correct chart. All the students change their chart to match this one.
5 When all students have the same chart, assign each student a box or boxes, according to class numbers.
6 Ask each student to study the part of the text that is relevant to their box.
7 Take the texts back.
8 Point to the chart on the board. Begin with the first box and ask the student who was assigned that box to explain what happens. Point to the next box to elicit the next part from the appropriate student and so on. If you come to branches or alternatives, guide the class down the one you want to take first. The class thus recount the text as a group.
9 Repeat, reassign the boxes and repeat again.

1.13

LEVEL
Elementary+

FOCUS
Drawing flow charts, discussing the argument of a text

MATERIALS
Class sets of two texts

WAYS WITH FLOW CHARTS 2

This is an activity for students who have some experience of the flow chart idea.

SUGGESTED TEXTS

Two texts describing different processes, procedures or dilemmas or two texts with narrative progression or argument.

Preparation

1 Divide the class into two groups.
2 Give each member of Group 1 a copy of one text, and each member of Group 2 a copy of the other. They read the texts.
3 Each group prepares a blank flow chart of their text, making one copy for every two students in a group.
4 Groups exchange blanks and texts.
5 Each group completes the other's flow chart. They should discuss this so that every student in the group gets the same result.
6 Each group appoints 'a conductor'. The conductor from Group 1 draws their group's original blank chart on the board then asks Group 2 to label it.
7 The conductor talks Group 2 through the flow chart, asking them to recount the text.
8 Group 2 appoint a conductor who leads Group 1 through Group 2's blank chart.

1.14

LEVEL
Elementary+

FOCUS
Drawing flow charts, discussing the argument of a text

MATERIALS
Class set of a text

WAYS WITH FLOW CHARTS 3

In this exercise the flow chart is like a skeleton that is slowly fleshed out by the text.

SUGGESTED TEXT

A text describing different processes, procedures or dilemmas or a text with narrative progression or argument.

Preparation

Draw a complete flow chart of the text. Make a class set.

Procedure

1 Hand out a copy of the flow chart to each student.
2 Write on the board, in a random pattern, the words or phrases which you think most relevant to the labels of the chart. Deal with pronunciation and problems of meaning as you write them up.

3 Put the students into pairs. Tell them that the words on the board elaborate on the labels in the chart. Tell them to cluster the words round the box in the flow chart that they seem to go with. For some words the match will be clear, with others it may be a more random process.

4 Hand out the texts and ask students to read them and cluster the words correctly.

5 Take the text back and ask students to tell you about it with the help of the flow chart and the clusters.

TEXTUAL CARDIOGRAMS

While flow charts may help students to express the central argument or theme of a text, graphs are useful for helping students measure their own responses to what is on the page.

This activity is an adaptation of one for helping students respond to video. Students discuss their emotional reactions to what they read. It can be a useful way to engage their interest at a first reading.

SUGGESTED TEXT

Any with a strong and variable emotional content, climactic scenes from stories or plays, also poems.

Procedure

1 Explain that you are going to draw a line graph which registers the 'heartbeat' of a scene with its emotional peaks, troughs, and jagged edges. This graph is a 'textual cardiogram'.

The following text is from Jane Austen's *Pride and Prejudice*.

Elizabeth was suddenly roused by the sound of the doorbell, and her spirits were a little fluttered by the idea of its being Colonel Fitzwilliam himself, who had once before called late in the evening, and might now come to enquire particularly after her. But this idea was soon banished, and her spirits were very differently affected, when, to her utter amazement, she saw Darcy walk into the room. Elizabeth was surprised but said not a word. After a silence of several minutes he came towards her in an agitated manner, and thus began, 'In vain have I struggled. It will not do. My feelings will not be repressed. You must allow me to tell you how ardently I admire and love you.'

Elizabeth's astonishment was beyond expression. She started, coloured, doubted, and was silent.

Jane Austen, *Pride and Prejudice* Pan 1967 p141

1.15

LEVEL
Intermediate+

FOCUS
Discussing and expressing feelings, relating actions to states of mind, mime, recounting past events

MATERIALS
Class set of a text

This text might give the following cardiogram:

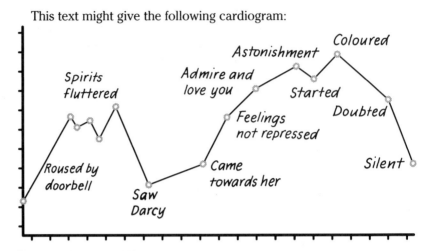

© Longman Group UK Ltd 1991

2 Give each student a copy of the text and ask them to read it and make a cardiogram of it.

3 Ask each student to label the most distinctive points on the graph with the appropriate phrases from the text.

4 Put the students into groups of three or four and ask them to compare their graphs and discuss any differences.

5 Ask students to illustrate the phrases on their cardiogram by mime or by recounting real or imaginary moments that gave them similar feelings. Who does what should be a matter of choice and the whole class may opt for one system. The rest of the class should guess the words that are being illustrated. If students want to dwell on moments that were important to them then allow them to discuss these with the class.

6 Students exchange cardiograms then reread the text while looking at their partner's graph. This may help them to view the text differently.

VARIATIONS

The cardiogram does not only have to express the emotional development of a text. It can have a much wider application when applied to any of the following aspects. Step 5 should be omitted when using these variations.

1 The student's own degree of interest or involvement in the text.
   The words on the cardiogram can show the points in the reading that most grab or repel. This type of graph can be a very good way for students to deal with their indifference to the reading matter that a course may inflict upon them. Teachers should sometimes be prepared for graphs that dip, or bump along a bottom line, but a labelling of the troughs of indifference can help the teacher to discover why students react as they do. The formulation of a negative opinion is as valid a language learning activity as any other.

2 The student's view of how original or insightful the text is.
   This can work very well with articles on current affairs.

3 The student's view of how much the text teaches them.

The graph provides a scale of novelty and shows whether the text is merely telling them what they already know or is stating something new. It can also chart the movement of a text from the restating of old knowledge towards the communication of something new. This is particularly good for technical or scientific texts dealing with new developments.

ACKNOWLEDGEMENT

The idea of the emotion graph was first applied to scenes from videos and comes to me from Peter Lavery.

ROUTE VIGNETTES

This activity is like a halfway house between the representation of text through a diagram and the fuller expression of meaning that is possible with pictures. It exploits the old diagram dictation technique, with the text as the source for the dictation, but involves students in the more interesting and entertaining process of setting out, not a straight map but a series of route vignettes. It puts the text into play in a communicative way and is particularly useful in ESP classes.

Pause lines are used to allow control over the speed at which students read the text and to encourage students to listen to each section.

SUGGESTED TEXT

Descriptions of a device, of a place or places or of a journey through places.

Preparation

1 On your master copy of the text draw pause lines (/ /) before an item in the text that refers to a physical feature of the place or of the thing being described. The following example for elementary students makes this clear:

At first you walk along a dark path where / / rain sometimes drips on you from the trees. The path opens out before it passes along / / the bottom of a small canyon between huge rocks. At the end of the path there is a / / wooden gate through which you can see / / a wood in the distance. On the left there is / / the entrance to a cave in the walls of the canyon. If you go into the cave, you wind along / / a narrow passage decorated on each side with / /pictures of strange gods. / /Lights burn in front of the pictures. At the end of the passage you come out onto a / / terrace cut into the side of the rock. This terrace looks over / / a large lake. In the middle of the lake there is / / an island with / / a pagoda on it.

© Longman Group UK Ltd 1991

2 Make a class set of the texts with pause marks.

1.16

LEVEL
Elementary+

FOCUS
Reading out loud, listening, diagram dictation

MATERIALS
Class set of a text

Procedure

1 Divide the class into two groups, one of readers and one of map-makers. Readers and map-makers sit together in pairs. The readers have copies of the text and the map-makers have blank sheets of paper.

2 Check that every word after the pause lines is understood.

3 Ask the readers to read the text out loud while the map-maker draws a map or diagram of the place or device mentioned in the text. The reader must pause at the pause marks so that the map-maker has enough time to draw in each new feature. For example, using the text on page 25 the reader reads: 'At first you walk along a dark path where', and the map-maker draws:

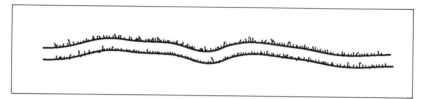

The reader continues: 'rain sometimes drips on you from the trees' and the map-maker draws:

The reader should not repeat sentences or give any help other than the pause that the map-maker needs. The first map will probably not be complete.

4 The reader and map-maker exchange roles. The new map-maker will use their partner's diagram to help them recount the text which they have just read. If they fail because of bad memory, bad comprehension or a bad map, the reader can use the text to help out. The map-maker can amend the map if necessary.

5 Students put their maps and texts away.

6 One student comes to the board to transcribe a map of the text that the class will collectively dictate. Discussion and argument will ensue. For example:

Student 1	You go along a narrow passage.
Student 2	No, wind along. The narrow passage winds.
Map-maker	Wind or go?
Class	Wind.

7 All students reread the text.

VARIATION 1

This provides the same treatment for short narrative texts.

1 Explain the idea of a narrative as a 'journey through time'. The main events are the places that a person passes through. To clarify, draw the vignettes of your own life on the board.

2 Get students to draw the main events of their lives then to explain these life maps to a neighbour.

3 Proceed from Step 1 of the original activity.

DRAWING A TEXT

The free use of drawing in this activity allows for personal interpretation and becomes a way for students to formulate their own responses to a text. I have used this activity in multicultural ESL classes where the exercise is an interesting way to show how a simple item like a river can be viewed in different ways thus raising questions about the true meanings of words. Remember that bad drawings can make the activity better by forcing a student to explain their inadequate picture. 'I can't draw' is therefore no excuse. The exercise is useful for ESP classes, particularly for descriptions of systems.

1.17

LEVEL
Elementary+

FOCUS
Drawing, discussing impressions and associations

MATERIALS
Class set of a text, Blu-tack or sellotape

SUGGESTED TEXT

Description of a device, an apparatus, a place or places.

Preparation

1 List and count the individual noun features in the descriptive text. If the description is of a building these might be the doors, windows, surroundings or rooms. Decide how many features to highlight.

Procedure

1 Tell the students the first feature of the text and ask them to draw it.

2 Students look at each other's drawings.

3 Students exchange drawings with a partner.

4 Students give their partner a mark out of five for artistic ability. The assessment is fairly serious and marks should not be given randomly.

5 Students circulate around the class and discuss their marks and pictures. They could say why they drew things the way they did. They could complain about their mark to someone else.

6 Appoint two readers and give them the text. The readers will be the students with the lowest marks for art. If you have a class of more than twenty, appoint three readers.

7 Explain the idea of an important feature, animal, person or object.

8 The readers scan the text for mention of features, objects, animals, etc. When a reader finds one, they read it out loud and assign it to an artist to be drawn. The readers should try to keep all the artists busy and they could give the same feature to two or three. Intervene to make sure this happens.

9 Artists discuss how they imagined the thing that they drew and how they would have liked to have drawn it if they could draw better.

10 Students pass their pictures around so that everyone sees everyone else's picture. Students who do not understand a picture can ask the artist for an explanation.

11 Distribute the text for reading by everyone.

12 Artists tell the class if their knowledge of the text would make them draw their feature differently.

13 One student sticks their picture on the board or wall. The others locate theirs around it to make a collage or comic strip that tells the story of the text.

VARIATION 1

For narrative texts or descriptions of procedures and processes.

1 When preparing the text, concentrate on key events instead of key features. For example for a sentence like 'I arrived at the old gate', the drawing should not be just of a gate but of a person arriving at one.

VARIATION 2

For texts combining narration and description.

1 Treat key features and key events separately. For example, the following text would give the key events and features listed below it.

I arrived at the old gate and passed into the city. I found the Blue Bell Inn and went in. The tap room was low and long. It had huge wooden barrels at one end and a log fire at the other. There were a few customers asleep under the tables.

Key events	Key features
arrive at old gate	long, low tap room
into city	huge wooden barrels
find Inn	log fire
	customers asleep under tables

2 At Step 13 assemble the pictures in the order of the narrative. Some key features may break down into smaller parts as the scene shifts from place to place. These can be assembled round the thing they are a part of. The pictures of the barrels, the fire and customers would thus be clustered around the one of the tap room.

REINVENTING WRITING

1.18

LEVEL
Elementary+

FOCUS
Skimming,
discussing a text,
drawing diagrams

MATERIALS
Class sets of two
texts, Plain paper
or card

Drawing can be used not only to focus understanding upon key features of the text but on its detail as well. This activity gets students to fumble after a word-for-word reproduction of the part of a text they have never seen! The task may appear too great a challenge but is only really so for the teacher more interested in a perfect result than in a lively interactive lesson that gets students using and thinking about a text.

SUGGESTED TEXT
Any two short texts of not more than three hundred words. These can be extracts from the same piece or a longer text divided into two parts.

Preparation

1 Divide the text into two halves as with the following example for advanced students:

The Loss of Biological Diversity

Part 1

The lost potential of the earth's biological resourses is often neglected in considering the consequences of deforestation in the tropics. Tropical forests contain both the richest variety and the least well-known flora and fauna in the world. It would be difficult to overstate the potential value of this huge stock of biological capital. If carefully managed, this capital could be a rich sustainable source of building materials and fuel, as well as medicinal plants, speciality woods, nuts and fruits.

Part 2

However, if present trends continue, sustained benefits from this capital will never be realised. Unique local plants and animals will be unknowingly and carelessly destroyed. Particularly well-adapted and fast-growing local trees will be cut before their fruits and seeds are collected. In short, the projected loss of tropical forests represents a massive expenditure of biological capital, an expenditure so large and sudden that it will surely limit the future benefits from even a careful husbanding of the remaining biotic resources of the earth.

Gerald O'Barney *The Global 2000 Report to the President* Blue Angel Inc. 1981 p329

2 Cut the paper or card into lots of small, word-size pieces

Procedure

1 Divide the class into two groups. Give each group a set of either Part 1 or Part 2 texts.

2 Each group reads through their text and circles the noun phrases and verb phrases in each sentence. Students should understand that for noun phrases they can circle an article, an adjective and a noun, such as *the lost potential, the earth's biological resources*, or even an entire subject phrase together, such as *the lost potential of the earth's biological resources*.

3 Tell the class they are going to reinvent pictorial or hieroglyphic writing and must represent each noun phrase or verb phrase with a single diagram or picture. They should try to make this picture comprehensible to someone who has never seen it before. Students should not draw a whole sentence as a single diagram because this will discourage them from analysing the text in detail. Explain that they should write one hieroglyph on each card and make the difference between noun and verb phrases clear by marking them with an N or a V.

4 Before they start, each group should decide how they will organise this task since there will not be enough time for all students to do all of the text. They could give one or more sentences to each student, for example. Time is limited so they have to be efficient.

5 Hand out the blank cards and ask each group to write their hieroglyphs on them.

6 Each group sets out their hieroglyphic text in front of them. They could arrange it in columns, or in lines going from right to left or from left to right.

7 The groups swap places. They should now be able to read each other's hieroglyphs.

8 Students from the first group take turns to try to read the hieroglyphs of the second group. The second group can help them but with mime and gesture only.

9 Repeat with the second group reading the hieroglyphs of the first group.

10 The groups exchange texts. They use the texts to make a correct interpretation of the hieroglyphs.

11 Each group takes back its own hieroglyphs and shuffles them. Each group now tries to use the hieroglyphs to make a sentence or two that is not in the text. They cannot change the meaning of their hieroglyphs but they may have to invent a few more to make a new sentence.

PICTURE CLOZE

1.19

LEVEL
Lower
intermediate+

FOCUS
Work study,
skimming, orally
reconstructing a
text

MATERIALS
Class set of any
text, blank paper,
Blu-tack and
correction fluid

This activity helps students to scan text for particular items, to remember difficult vocabulary and to orally reconstruct text.

Preparation

1 Find all the words or short phrases in the text which you think will cause the class problems. You will need at least one such word or phrase for every sentence of text so you may have to find items which the students now know but which have caused problems before.
2 List this lexis in random order on the board.

Procedure

1 Point to a lexical item on the board, call out a student's name and ask them to write this item down. Repeat until all the students have an item or until you have given them all out.
2 Give each student a piece of blank paper and ask them to make a quick drawing or diagram of their word. Help if they have problems with meaning or allow them to use a dictionary. Explain that not all words can be represented directly. *Walk* may have to be shown through a picture of someone walking, *Heat* through a fire, etc.
3 In random order, ask the students to stick their pictures on the board, number them and explain them to the class.
4 Hand a copy of the text to each student.
5 Explain that everyone should work individually and race each other to write the number of the appropriate picture against its word in the text.
6 Ask students to delete all the numbered words from their text.
7 Rearrange the pictures on the board in random order and delete the numbers.
8 Call one student to the board.
9 Choose a student to read the text. Explain that they should say a silly word like 'rabbit' when they come to a deleted word. Ask the student at the board to number the picture that matches the deleted word. The pictures are thus ordered according to their occurrence in the text.
10 Take the texts back.
11 Point to a picture and ask the students if they can remember the matching word, then ask them to suggest an appropriate sentence for the word that is based upon the one in the text. Do not attempt to elicit the sentence exactly as it is in the text. A rough paraphrase that makes sense of the picture is all that you can hope for. Repeat with the other pictures.
12 Divide the class into pairs. Ask the partners to tell the text to each other with the help of the pictures.

CHAPTER 2

Giving words meaning

These activities deal closely with the actual language of the text. They are to help students understand and remember the words on the page. They aim to make students think about how words combine as sentences and sentences as text to convey a larger meaning. Their intention is to get students to read faster and more accurately and also to enrich their spoken language.

The emphasis is first on how sentences combine to give the overall meaning of the text. It then narrows towards the sentences themselves and finally to the very words out of which those sentences are built.

2.1 SCRAMBLED OPTIONS

A scrambled text is one cut into sections and then mixed up. It is a well-tried way to reduce a text to more manageable parts and thus to make it more presentable to the class. Scrambling also teaches an appreciation of some of the other elements that change written statements into text.

All text is discourse, that is to say, it is a series of sentences which are moulded into an argument and made to cohere. Cutting up a text then putting it back together enhances a student's ability to understand the techniques a language uses to fit sentences together. It also fosters an understanding of the overall thrust and direction of a text's meaning and detracts from too great an emphasis on the sense of separate sentences or words.

There are basically three formulae for the scrambled activities to use in EFL classes. All put the language of the text into play in the class but with different degrees of control.

Preparing scrambled copies of a text need not be time-consuming if you use this technique:
- Cut one text into the required number of sections.
- Paste the pieces onto backing paper, with clear divisions between the pieces.
- Photocopy these papers, then cut them up at the divisions.

METHOD 1
Here the language used by students is not closely guided by that in the text and the emphasis is strongly on subject matter. The main task involves the assembly of a group summary. It can be done with any text of any level and runs broadly as follows:
1 The class is divided into groups of between four and eight. The groups should be larger for longer texts and smaller for shorter ones.

2 The text is cut into as many pieces as there are students in each group. Each piece should make complete sense. Do not cut through sentences.

3 Do not give out the complete texts. Give each learner in the group one section for study. Each group should have the entire text between them, though they must not read each other's sections.

4 Allow the class fifteen minutes (more or less according to the length and complexity of the text) to collect all the information they can about the text from other members of their group. Encourage them to move around and to exchange information about their particular section.

5 Take back the sections of the text.

6 Then either the students go away and individually write a summary of the text (for a writing exercise), or they make written or oral summaries of the text in pairs (for a communication and a writing exercise).

7 All students receive a complete copy of the text for silent individual reading to check their summaries.

METHOD 2

This technique involves the entwining of one text with one or more others. This can be done with any texts of any level and there are two basic methods. The first involves the kind of cut and summary technique outlined above. The second involves a closer reading and the assembly of smaller pieces.

For the first approach you will need two or more texts of a similar length and type, such as two texts about the lives of two different kings, one text about the two stroke cycle and one about the four stroke cycle (for ESP classes), short descriptions of the French and Russian Revolutions, two different dessert recipes, two poems by the same poet, etc.

The preparation and in-class procedures are as follows:

1 Cut both the texts into as many pieces as there are students. If some of the pieces are larger than one paragraph, cut them again and give some students two pieces of text, but no one should be given two consecutive pieces from the same text.

2 Allow students approximately fifteen minutes (depending on the complexity of the texts) to collect all the information they can about the two texts. Tell them to move around the class, forming groups to exchange information about the content of the individual sections.

3 Ask each group to make oral or written summaries of the two texts. (You can, if you wish, provide the title of the texts at this point.)

4 Give every student a copy of the complete text for rapid reading.

The second approach requires students to make a closer study of the text, since it is divided into smaller pieces.

1 Cut both texts into separate, but complete, sentences. Put the parts together in a scrambled order to make one nonsensical text out of the two.

2 Prepare one copy of the jumbled text per student and one copy of each original text per student.

3 Give out the jumbled texts. Ask the students to work in pairs and to attempt to sort the jumbled text into two texts that make sense. It is sometimes useful to indicate the first line of each text.

4 Each student finds a different partner. The new pair compares their two versions of the texts, perhaps by reading them out loud to each other or by saying what they are about.

5 Give out the two original texts. The students then compare their versions with the originals.

METHOD 3

This is really a reading out loud and listening comprehension exercise. It also helps to create an understanding of how sentences hang together as discourse. It works well with any text at any level. The length of the text depends on the number of students but there should be between one and two sentences per student.

1 Cut the text into as many pieces as there are students. The pieces can be cut across both paragraphs and sentences, so the cutting can ignore any idea of complete sense as in the following example for elementary students:

He sits near the window all day. He never

---
goes out and he never leaves

---
his seat. He watches everyone but he talks

---
to no one. He remembers everything he

---
sees and some children call

---
him 'the camera'. At night he is still there. The light

---
from the street lamp makes his face yellow like

---
old paper. We are afraid of him because he keeps our lives

---
shut in his head. This is why we look

---
after him and give him food.

© Longman Group UK Ltd 1991

1 Give one piece of text to each student.

2 The students practise reading their sections to themselves, concentrating on fluency and pronunciation. Clear up any comprehension problems if the cutting makes this possible.

3 Ask the student who thinks they have the first part of the text to read it to the class. Then ask for the second section to be read, then the third and so on, until the whole text has been read out in order.

4 Repeat the reading at a faster pace. Make sure that every student comes in on time.

5 Take the pieces back, shuffle and redistribute them.
6 Get a section by section reading as before. Try to get the reading as seamless as possible, with no pauses between the sections.
7 Repeat Steps 5 & 6 if you like.
8 Distribute copies of the text for rapid silent reading.

SCRAMBLED OPTION 1
THE WHISPERED JIGSAW

This activity is based on the old Chinese Whispers game and is a useful way to make the interpretation of text controversial and thus encourage students to use its new language.

Preparation

Prepare class sets of a text cut into four to eight pieces. The class will be divided into groups of between four and eight so the text should be cut according to group numbers. You will need one set of cut text for each group.

Procedure

1 Divide the class into circles of no more than eight.
2 Each student takes one piece of the text for study.
3 After each student has read their piece, take it back.
4 Working from left to right, each student exchanges the content of their piece with their neighbour in the circle.
5 Then, each student repeats to the person on their right what they heard from the person on their left.
6 Repeat and continue until everybody in the circle has heard a version of every section of the text.
7 Each student writes a summary of the text in note form.
8 One student tells their summary to the rest of their group. Others can interrupt and correct if necessary. Let the group argue about what the text actually says.
9 Hand out the complete text for reading. Ask students to say where they got the text right or wrong.

2.2

LEVEL
Elementary+

FOCUS
Listening to summaries, discussing and disagreeing

MATERIALS
Class set of any text

2.3

LEVEL
Intermediate+

FOCUS
Inventing and describing text, persuading, negotiating

MATERIALS
Class set of any text

SCRAMBLED OPTION 2
THE TEXT MARKET

This is an activity for lovers of argument, barter, pandemonium and deceit. Recently I found it reawakened tribal enmities in a group. All good language practice at least!

Preparation

1 Cut the text into eight or ten pieces. Provide enough cut copies of the text for each student to be able to put together one complete version.

Procedure

1 Shuffle the pieces of text and put them in a pile in the middle of the class.
2 Ask students to select pieces at random so that they each have an equal number of extracts.
3 Students study the content of their text pieces, some of which will be the same. In order to complete their text they will have to exchange those that are surplus for those that are not.
4 Tell the students that in order to exchange, they will have to sell their unwanted pieces as if they are in a market. They will shout about the pieces they have got, describing what they are about. The only rule of the text market is that text pieces cannot be shown before they are exchanged. Students can therefore lie about what they are selling. They can invent the description of the piece they are selling in order to make somebody want it. This tactic is effective if the customer is not sure what the complete text is going to look like. They could also describe a piece they want to keep then give away one that is quite different.
5 When students accumulate a complete text, they sit out and study it. Any students who have the complete text from the beginning can help others. They can help by describing the complete text to those who are looking for pieces. If they hear somebody selling a fake section of text they might call this person a cheat. On the other hand they might also call an honest person a cheat and make trade even more difficult!
6 The chaos will probably resolve itself eventually. If it shows no sign of reaching a conclusion, you can intervene, expose the cheats and then introduce people to others with whom they can do an honest trade.

SCRAMBLED OPTION 3
THE ASSEMBLY LINE RACE

2.4

LEVEL
Elementary+

FOCUS
Reading for gist,
talking about text,
putting text
together

MATERIALS
Class set of any
text

A straightforward and fast pace exercise, which is good for waking up classes to discourse on a drowsy day.

Preparation

Cut the text into small pieces of not more than two sentences long. Cut through both paragraphs and sentences. The segments that you give to the class should be rectangular. They should not fit together jigsaw fashion. This means either retyping the sections to make one separate from the other or sticking the segments onto backing paper then photocopying them and cutting the photocopy. The class will be divided into teams of four to six, so prepare one cut copy of the text for each team.

Procedure

1 Divide the class into teams of four to six.
2 Give each team all the shuffled pieces of the text.
4 The teams race each other to assemble the text in the right order.
5 The teams compare their assembled versions.
6 Distribute the complete text for rapid reading.

SCRAMBLED OPTION 4
ASKING ABOUT THE TEXT

2.5

LEVEL
Elementary+

FOCUS
Writing and
answering
questions, making
summaries

MATERIALS
Class set of any
text

A more interesting and more communicative way to do the old question and answer reading comprehension.

Preparation

Cut the text into as many sections as there are students. The cutting should be into topic areas, as far as possible. Each section should make complete sense. If your text will not stretch round the whole class when cut, then divide the class into two and cut two copies of the text.

Procedure

1 Distribute all the sections of the text. Each student should have at least one section. Some students may have two.
2 Students individually write the question or questions that will best elicit the content of their portion of the text. Help by giving them appropriate question cues (interrogatives or auxiliaries).

3 The students circulate, orally collecting and correcting other students' questions. Each student should copy down everybody else's questions.
4 In pairs, the students write speculative answers to the questions.
5 The students put their piece of text into a pile in the middle of the class and take a different one.
6 In pairs, they decide which question their new piece of text answers and correct their speculative reply accordingly.
7 They continue to exchange pieces until they know the answers to all the questions.
8 Students use the information gained to write collective or group summaries of the text.
9 Give out the text and ask students to compare their summaries with the text itself.

2.6

LEVEL
Elementary+

FOCUS
Translating from L1 to TL and vice versa, reading out loud

MATERIALS
Class set of any text, Blu-tack

SCRAMBLED OPTION 5
SCRAMBLED TRANSLATIONS

Translation is often now considered to be an activity that does not teach students a language so much as the skill of translation itself. However, translation is often still a course requirement. It also plays an essential role in language learning since all students move between their L1 (first language) and the TL (target language) and only the strict behaviourist would regard this as a practice that should be stamped out at all costs.

This activity gives a lively slant to translation. It involves students in the two way process of changing TL into L1 and L1 into TL. The TL is always predominant. As in any good language learning activity you do not need to know any of the L1s in the class for this to be a success. It works best if two or more students in the class share the same L1. Monolingual classes are easiest but not necessarily the most interesting.

Remember that many students still enjoy translation because it helps them get a longer lasting grip on elusive structures and vocabulary.

Preparation

1 Cut the text into meaningful sections. Try to have one section for each student. If the text is short, think about dividing your class into two groups and cut the text according to group size.

Procedure

1 Give each student one section of the text.
2 Ask everyone to write a translation of their section of the text in their own language.

3 Ask each student to exchange their translation with a partner with the same L1. If you have any students who do not share their L1 with anyone else, they could translate back their own translations after the original text has been taken away.

4 Ask each student to turn their partner's (or their own, if working alone) translation back into English. This translation should be on a separate piece of paper. Circulate, trying to correct as many as possible.

5 Ask the class, 'Who has translated back the beginning of the text please? Read out your version.' Then 'Who has the second section? Read it please.' And so on until the end of the text. Intervene as you go to correct the English.

6 Repeat the reading at a faster pace. Make sure that every student comes in on time.

7 Take the pieces back, reshuffle and redistribute them.

8 Try to get a section-by-section reading with no pauses between the sections.

9 Students stick up their translations in order on the board. Everyone comes to the board for another reading of this complete version of the text.

10 Distribute the original text for reading. Students compare their version with the original.

SCRAMBLED OPTION 6
OPPOSITES

2.7

LEVEL
Lower intermediate+

This activity helps students read text with a more detailed understanding, expand their vocabulary and grasp what is meant by 'opposite sense'. The idea of an 'opposite' is not always easy to grasp and the search for one can force students to immerse themselves more fully in the language of the text and the TL in general. If you try the activity yourself, you will understand how involving it can be. Do not hope for perfect results – the process of doing this exercise is just as interesting as the outcome.

FOCUS
Note-taking, changing sentences to their opposites

MATERIALS
Class set of any text

Preparation

1 Scramble the text into as many parts as you have students. Each part must make complete sense, as in the example on page 40 for lower intermediate students. If you have more students than sentences, plan to split the class into two groups.

The Crocodile

I sat down with her.

We watched the river beneath.

'It's a deep river,' she said, quietly.

'And dangerous,' I said.

'Why?'
'Crocodiles,' I said and looked up at the sky.

'Crocodiles in Scotland?' She was nearly surprised.

'Well, yes, you see,' but I couldn't finish.

'Look,' she screamed. It came slowly towards us, a great green crocodile in a kilt.

We were outside her house.

'I see things with you,' she said, then kissed me goodbye.

Procedure

1 Give each student their section of scrambled text.
2 Ask each student to rewrite their section so that it means exactly the opposite to what it says. Students must consider carefully the meaning of opposite. This is not a question of changing negatives to positives but of making right into left or inside into outside. Straight changes from positive to negative or negative to positive should not be allowed or should be strictly limited. Students must try to retain normal sense. A model answer from the example text 'The Crocodile' might be as follows:

I stood up and went away from her. We turned our eyes from the lake above us.
'It's a shallow lake,' she shouted.
'And so safe,' I said.
'Why?'
'No tadpoles,' I said and looked down at the ground.
'Tadpoles in England?' She was terribly surprised.
'Well, yes, you don't understand,' I concluded.
'Shut your eyes,' she whispered quietly. It went slowly away from us, a tiny black tadpole in tweed trousers.
We were inside her flat.
'I am blind with you,' she wrote, then shook my hand in greeting.
© Longman Group UK Ltd 1991

This model is better than you are likely to get from your students but is worth giving as an example of what to aim for. Make clear, however, that students cannot expect to find opposites for everything in the text.

3 Ask students to read out their altered section in turn. The rest of the class writes what they say in note form.

4 Students form groups of three and try to reconstruct the original meaning of the text.

5 Hand out the original text and ask students to read it. Allow them a limited time.

6 Ask the student with the first section to read their opposite again. Students follow the original text and decide whether the opposite version was correct and offer alternatives.

VARIATION
With elementary classes, simply ask the students to change negatives to positives or positives to negatives. This can also have very amusing results.

SCRAMBLED OPTION 7
FINDING YOUR PART

This type of activity is very text specific in that it requires a text in the form of a dialogue. However, dialogues and conversations abound in EFL textbooks at all levels and this is a useful and entertaining way for students to come to grips with such texts. The activity also works well for more advanced students of literature.

SUGGESTED TEXT
A dialogue or conversation between several people who have recognisable character types, a short play, a scene or a meaningful extract from a play.

Preparation

1 Read the script so you can tell the students a little about each of the characters and can set the scene. If you have an extract from a longer play you may also need to say something about the context or the story preceding the extract.

2 Rewrite your script so that it reads as a continuous piece of prose with no indication of which character is speaking. Stage directions should be omitted. The example on page 42 is a short melodrama for elementary students. In this play the action is straightforward and the students would need to know only that the characters are:
Maureen a rich lady of leisure; Bertram, her simple teenage son; Jason, the Butler; Stephen, Maureen's lover and her husband's best friend; Paul, Maureen's rich husband.

3 Make one copy of the scrambled script on page 43 for each student.

2.8

LEVEL
Elementary+

FOCUS
Matching conversation to character and context, acting out a script

MATERIALS
Class set of a text, tape recorder or video camera (optional)

Afternoon tea: a play for five characters

Enter the Butler

Butler   Mr Jennings, Madam.

Maureen   Thank you Jason, show him in and bring some tea.

Exit Butler. Enter Stephen with force and passion

Stephen   Maureen, Maureen, I had to see you –

Maureen   For heaven's sake, somebody will hear!

Enter the idiot son, Bertram

Bertram   Mother, mother, I can't find my bedroom.

Stephen   I don't care! I can't keep the secret any more!

Maureen   Oh Bertram, go and find Jason.

Bertram   I can't find him either. Who is that strange man? Why is he taking his coat off?

Maureen   Please don't. Don't Stephen, not now.

Enter Butler

Butler   Ahem.

Maureen   Ah yes. The tea. Now please show the master where his bedroom is.

Exit the Butler leading Bertram.

Stephen   Oh God! Alone at last.

Maureen   Really not now. He's – ah –

Enter Paul in a wet raincoat

Paul   What horrible weather!

Maureen   My God!

Paul   You, Stephen, you, of all people!

Stephen   I – I –

Maureen   No, no, no for God's sake.

Bertram   I lost Jason and I can't find it. What is that man doing to Papa?

Paul picks up the poker from the fireplace and rushes at Stephen

Stephen   Oh, my God, don't.

Maureen   Paul no! No! Oh you brute! What have you done!

Paul   He had it coming to him.

Maureen   Oh he's –

Paul   Yes, he is; the swine.

Enter the Butler

Butler   Ahem.

Bertram   That man's lazy. He must get up.

Maureen   Oh heavens I wish he could!

© Longman Group UK Ltd 1991

Procedure

1 Divide the class into groups. Each group should have the same number of students as there are characters in the play. If the class does not divide exactly, give some students two parts.

2 Assign each student a part. Tell them who their character is and what they are like.

3 Distribute the scrambled scripts and ask each student, individually to try to find their part, and then write the name or initials of their character above the places where they start speaking.

4 When students have finished, ask each group to act out the script without talking about it first. The result can often be hilarious with students saying each other's lines or not coming in on cue.

5 Distribute the real scripts for reading and comparison.

EXTENSION

Record or video performances of the correct script or even of the students' different versions if they sound better!

Scrambled Script

Mr Jennings, Madam. Thank you Jason, show him in and bring some tea. Maureen, Maureen, I had to see you. For heaven's sake, somebody will hear! Mother, mother, I can't find my bedroom. I don't care! I can't keep the secret any more! Oh, Bertram, go and find Jason. I can't find him either. Who is that strange man? Why is he taking his coat off? Please don't. Don't Stephen, not now. Ahem. Ah yes. The tea. Now, please show the master where his bedroom is. Ah! Alone at last. Really not now. He's – ah – What horrible weather! My God! You, Stephen, you of all people. I–I No, no, no for God's sake. I lost Jason and I can't find it. What is that man doing to Papa? Oh, my God, don't. Paul no! No! Oh you brute! What have you done! He had it coming to him. Oh he's – Yes, he is; the swine. Ahem. That man's lazy. He must get up. Oh heavens, I wish he could!

© Longman Group UK Ltd 1991

EMPTY WORDS, EMPTY VESSELS

An understanding of the discourse of a text is critical to the understanding of the text itself. Scrambled activities get at the idea of discourse by asking students to assemble the different parts of the text. This activity develops an understanding of how text coheres when words are given meaning by those that come before or after them. The students' L1 may give them an instinctive grasp of this but the conscious development of such knowledge is a good way to help students find the gist of the text quickly and improve their reading fluency.

SUGGESTED TEXT

Any of short length, if possible double spaced.

2.9

LEVEL
Intermediate+

FOCUS
Analysing text, discussing meaning

MATERIALS
Class set of any short text, class set of sample text

Procedure

1 Give each student a copy of the text below. Students read it in pairs then suggest why some words are circled and joined together.

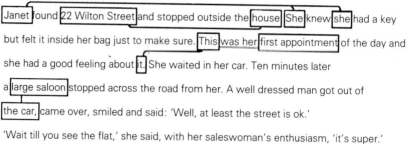

Janet found 22 Wilton Street and stopped outside the house. She knew she had a key but felt it inside her bag just to make sure. This was her first appointment of the day and she had a good feeling about it. She waited in her car. Ten minutes later a large saloon stopped across the road from her. A well dressed man got out of the car, came over, smiled and said: 'Well, at least the street is ok.'

'Wait till you see the flat,' she said, with her saleswoman's enthusiasm, 'it's super.'
© Longman Group UK Ltd 1991

2 Elicit or explain that the text illustrates how some words become meaningful because they refer back to others, thus *she* is meaningful in this text because it refers to Janet. Tell them that these words are 'empty vessels' until the text 'fills' them with meaning. Some empty words such as *this* can be filled by the sense of whole sentences.

3 Give out copies of the text to be studied. Ask students to show the relationship between words in the same way as in the example, by circling and joining together connected words.

4 Ask a student to begin reading the text out loud. When they come to a word that gets its meaning from another, the class interrupt and ask a question about it:

Student   Janet found 22 Wilton Street and stopped outside the house.
Class   What house?
Student   22 Wilton Street.

5 Continue in this way until the end of the text you are studying.

6 Ask the students to reread the text silently to consolidate their understanding of how it coheres.

7 Ask the students to work in pairs and to change the meanings of the empty words and thus what happens in the text. They do this by changing what the empty words refer to. Remind them that empty words can only be filled with certain things, thus *she* cannot refer to *man* but in some contexts it could be an animal. This is a possible rewriting of the first part of the example text.

Sue found (Ascot Place) and stopped outside the <u>house</u>. <u>She</u> knew <u>she</u> had (a pass) but felt <u>it</u> inside her bag just to make sure. <u>This</u> was (her first visit to the house) and <u>she</u> had a good feeling about <u>it</u>. She waited in her car. Ten minutes later (a small sports vehicle) stopped across <u>the road</u> from <u>her</u>. (A ragged youth) got out of <u>the car</u>, came over, smiled and said . . .

8 When they have finished, ask the students to find new partners and compare the changed texts by reading them to each other.

LOADED LANGUAGE, FULL VESSELS

2.10

LEVEL
Intermediate+

FOCUS
Reading for gist,
discussing
meaning,
elementary textual
analysis

MATERIALS
Class set of any
text, class set of
sample text

This activity asks students to focus on the way text coheres, not by using words whose meanings we know because of context, but because of our knowledge of the world. I call these words 'loaded nouns'. They are the vessels that we bring to the text already full of our own associations and meanings. The activity focuses on meaning, not in the sense of knowing that *tree* in one language is *arbre* in another, but in knowing the identity of the thing which the word *tree* or *arbre* represents. The activity is useful for helping students to remember the meanings of words and to read more fluently. It is useful if the class has previously done Activity 2.7 *Opposites.*

Preparation

1 To illustrate the procedure make one copy of the following under-lined text for each student or write it on the board.

> Now we'll discuss the Oix,' said Professor Baird. Jane, the girl with red <u>hair</u> looked out of <u>the window</u>. She was tired.
> 'A strange <u>creature</u>, the Oix,' the professor explained, he sounded nervous and began to talk faster. 'A large <u>head</u>, tiny <u>legs,</u> no <u>feet</u>, just <u>points</u> to stick in <u>things</u>.'
> Perhaps something was chasing him through his <u>lecture</u>. Jane felt a <u>pain</u>. It was Fergueson's <u>pencil-point</u> in her <u>side</u>.
> 'That's your Oix, my love,' Fergueson whispered angrily.
>
> © Longman Group UK Ltd 1991

Procedure

1 Distribute the text or ask the students to read it from the board. Ask them to discuss, in pairs, why some of the words are underlined and decide what these words have in common.
2 Try to lead students towards the idea that the underlined words are loaded nouns. We do not know their meaning because of information we have been given by the text but because of our own knowledge of the world. We have loaded them with associations of our own.
3 Give the students the text they are going to study. To check that they have an idea of a loaded noun ask them to identify a few.
4 Students read the text individually and underline the loaded nouns. Tell them not to worry about marking every one. They must only underline the items they do not understand. To do this they will have to try to puzzle out from the context whether an unknown word is a loaded noun or not.
5 When they have finished underlining, students can use dictionaries and ask for explanations or translations of the loaded nouns that are not understood.
6 Ask the students to tell you their loaded nouns and ask someone to write them up on the board in the order they appear in the text. Check that all meanings have been grasped by everyone.

7 Tell the students that you are going to say their name followed by a loaded noun. When they hear that word they must concentrate on it completely and think of the visual picture it creates. *A meal* to one person will be a steak and potatoes, to another a bowl of rice. Tell the students to think of every detail of their picture, even its smell.

8 Advise the students to close their eyes in order to concentrate better. Begin by saying a name then a loaded noun. Go round and round the class allocating all the words. Don't hurry. Students need time to build up their picture of one word before having to deal with another.

9 Say the loaded nouns or noun from the first sentence of the text and ask the students who thought about them/it to describe their pictures. If the pictures are blank, ask the class to help. Ask the class to read the first sentence and to decide whether or not the text influenced the speaker's picture of the word or the text would modify or completely change the word picture.

2.11

LEVEL
Intermediate+

FOCUS
Textual analysis, reading for gist, negotiating procedures

MATERIALS
Class set of any text

LOADED AND EMPTY

This activity combines the skills developed in the two previous ones (Activity 2.9 *Empty words, empty vessels* and Activity 2.10 *Loaded language, full vessels*) and should only be attempted after them.

Procedure

1 Divide the class into two teams.

2 Divide the board into two parts. Divide each part into two columns. Head one of the columns 'loaded' and the other 'empty'.

3 Explain that the loaded columns are for items which are meaningful to us because of our knowledge of the world and that the empty columns are for words which get their meaning by referring back to others in the text.

4 Give out copies of the text but tell the students not to look at them until you say 'go'.

5 Tell each team that they are going to scan the text in order to find as many words as possible for each category and that they are going to write these words into their appropriate column on the board. They will have a time limit for this. Allocate each team half of the board to write on. Words can be written down as many times as they appear in the text but must be numbered. If *it* occurs five times it can be written five times but as follows: *it*(1), *it*(2), *it*(3), etc. Students should not write up loaded words whose meanings they do not know nor empty words if they do not know what they refer to, or they will be penalised. If *it*(1) refers to a house and *it*(5) to a dog they must know this.

6 Give the teams a minute to decide how they are going to divide their task, then say 'go'.

7 Give the students the same time it takes you to find the words and scribble them down, then shout 'stop'.

8 One student from Team 1 reads a word from the list of Team 2 and asks any Team 2 member to either explain it or say what it refers to. They have ten seconds to answer. If they are wrong, delete that word from their side of the board.

9 Repeat with a student from Team 2 asking a Team 1 member to explain one of the words from their list.

10 Continue with different team members asking and answering each time.

11 Stop when each team has asked as many questions as the opposing team has words. If Team 1 has more words than Team 2, then Team 2 will ask more questions.

12 The winner is the team with the most words left on the board.

13 Ask students to reread the text to themselves, individually and more carefully.

THE AUTHOR AND THE ALIEN

2.12

LEVEL
Lower intermediate+

FOCUS
Reading for detailed understanding, expanding a text

MATERIALS
Class set of any text

This activity develops students' understanding of text as discourse by asking them to think about the knowledge they bring to the text in order to make sense of it and about what the text does not need to tell them. It is an interesting way to get students to think about how words mean what they do.

Procedure

1 Give each student a copy of the text.

2 Ask the students to imagine they are from another planet and that they have almost none of the knowledge of a human reader. They have literal translations for words but this does not really help because their own world is so different. For example in the sentence *I sat down and ate my meal* in the Western world *sit* generally assumes that there is a chair to sit on. It also sums up a series of actions – moving out the chair, walking round the chair, bending your knees, etc. In Arab society or in the Far East, *sit* might imply something quite different. *Meal* also implies a possible selection of food that will change according to the culture.

Ask the students to read the text and to think about some of the words that might cause them problems because of their alien knowledge. They should think about one or two words in every sentence.

3 Divide the students into pairs.

4 Explain that one partner is the writer of the text. They know everything about the text. The other is the alien who knows nothing.

The writer reads the text and stops after the first sentence. The alien asks them to explain in detail any item that seems difficult or strange.

5 Halfway through the text, the writer and the alien exchange roles.

6 When they have finished, assign each student a different sentence and ask them to write an expanded version of it, including all the extra information they extracted from their partner.

7 Ask them to read their expanded sentences out loud round the class, thus producing an expanded text.

ACKNOWLEDGEMENT
This activity is based on a discourse idea given to me by Seth Lindstromberg.

2.13

LEVEL
Elementary+

FOCUS
Reading and listening, asking questions, predicting

MATERIALS
Class set of any text

WHAT COMES NEXT? 1
TALKING OUT THE TEXT

The efficient reading of text not only needs a knowledge of the world (See Activity 2.10 *Loaded language, full vessels*), it also requires some sense of what the writer will say before they say it. Reading involves some prediction of meaning on the reader's part. As it unfolds an argument, text may be forever confirming or denying the reader's suppositions. There is a dialogue of confirmation and denial going on and this activity tries to improve understanding and concentrate on textual language by making the nature of that dialogue clear.

Preparation

1 Divide the text into two halves.

2 Think of points in every sentence of the text where you could stop a reading and get the listener to ask you a question about what comes next. Insert pause marks / / at these points.

Here is an example of a text which could be used by advanced students:

Dredgermen or Fishermen

These are men who are in the habit of coming out early in/ /the morning, as the tide may/ /suit, for the purpose of dredging from the bed of the/ /river coals which are occasionally spilled in weighing when being transferred into / /the barges.

If these parties are not successful in/ /getting coals there, they invariably go alongside of a loaded/ /barge and carry off/ /coals and throw a quantity of mud over them to make it appear as if/ /they had got them from the bed of the river. The police have made/ /numerous detections. Some have been imprisoned and others/ /have been transported.

Henry Mayhew, *London's Underworld*, William Kimber and Co., 1862, 1950, p.294

Procedure

1 Put the students into pairs and give each partner a different half of the text.
2 Tell the students that they are going to hear part of a text and that when the reading stops they must ask a question in order to find out what comes next. They are not to ask *wh-* type questions but the kind of intonation question where someone is asking for confirmation of what they already know. For example:

Teacher   These are men who are in the habit of coming out early in...?
Student   The evening?
Teacher   No, morning.

To be right a student does not have to suggest the exact words that come after the pause but just the overall sense. You do not always have to give straight corrections. You can answer with clues. For example:

Teacher   The police have made numerous...?
Student   Arrests?
Teacher   No, before an arrest.
Student   Discoveries?
Teacher   No, detections.

When the student has had a question answered, they should try to repeat a complete sentence or phrase as an intonation question:

Student   So they have made numerous discoveries?

Thus, bit by bit, the complete text is elicited as a kind of dialogue.
3 When the students have understood this, ask them to do the same in pairs. The student with the first part of the text will take the role of the teacher and the other will suggest continuations to the text.
4 Ask the students to change roles when they reach the second part of the text.
5 Ask students to find a new partner with the same part of the text.
6 Ask them to write some of their text in the question and answer dialogue form. They should just write a sentence or two.
7 The pairs with the first part of the text swap their dialogue with a pair with the second part.
8 Ask students to turn the dialogue back into a piece of straight text.
9 Again students with the first part of the text exchange with students who have the second part. Ask them to read the new part and compare it with what they have written.

ACKNOWLEDGEMENT
The idea of turning text into dialogue and dialogue back into text comes from Seth Lindstromberg.

2.14

LEVEL
Elementary –
intermediate

FOCUS
Listening to a
story, choral story-
telling

MATERIALS
Class set of a text

WHAT COMES NEXT? 2
PATTERN STORIES

This activity is based on students intervening in a reading of text to suggest what follows. The task is made much easier and more natural by a very specialised kind of text. The prediction process is really a way to involve the class in a collective and very traditional kind of story-telling. This is a lively and entertaining mix of listening and speaking which is less forced than the classic 'hear the story then tell it back' technique.

SUGGESTED TEXT

Stories where the plot consists of series of incidents that follow the same pattern. Each incident therefore becomes predictable. The following is an example based on an African folk tale:

African folk tale

A spirit went to his father and said:
'Father, I want to be alive.'
'That is complicated,' his father told him.
'To be alive you must first think, next you must remember, then you must feel, then smell, after that you must see, next hear and finally when you can do all these things you'll be alive.'
'How can I do this?' the spirit asked.
'Go and walk in the world,' said the father, 'and get what you can where you can.'

The spirit followed a path through the forest of the world and met a young man. The young man sat under a tree and frowned.
'Man,' said the spirit, 'please help me, I want to think.'
'To think, you need a mind,' said the man.
'Can I have your mind?' asked the spirit.
'Certainly,' said the man and after he gave away his mind he looked happy and young.
'Oh Father, help me,' the spirit suddenly cried in fear.
'Walk on through the world,' his father said, 'he who thinks also fears.'

The spirit came to a village and found an old man.
'Man,' said the spirit, 'please help me, I want to remember.'
'To remember you need a memory,' said the man.
'Can I have yours?' asked the spirit.
'Certainly,' said the man and after he gave away his memory he looked happy. The spirit looked at the path ahead but could not remember which way to go.
'Oh Father help me,' he cried.
'Walk on through the world,' his father said, 'he who remembers also forgets.'

The spirit came to a thorn tree and found a boy crying there.
'Man,' said the spirit, 'please help me, I want to feel.'
'To feel you need feelings,' said the boy.
'Can I have yours,' asked the spirit.
© Longman Group UK Ltd 1991

'Certainly,' said the young man and after he gave away his feelings he looked happy.

Then the spirit trod on a thorn.

'Ah,' he cried, 'Father help me.'

'Walk on through the world,' his father said, 'he who feels also feels pain.'

The spirit came to a dead animal and found a child sitting there holding his nose.

'Boy,' said the spirit, 'please help me, I want to smell things.'

'To smell you need a nose,' said the boy.

'Can I have yours?' asked the spirit.

'Certainly,' said the boy and took his hand away from his face.

The spirit smelt the dead animal and felt ill.

'Oh Father help me,' he cried.

'Walk on through the world,' his father said, 'he who smells must also smell bad things.'

The spirit came to dismal place without trees or flowers. He found a man there covering his eyes.

'Man,' said the spirit, 'please help me, I want to see.'

'To see you need eyes,' said the man.

'Can I have yours?' asked the spirit.

'Certainly,' said the man and smiled.

'Oh Father help me,' cried the spirit, 'this is a terrible world.'

'Walk on through it,' his father said, 'he who sees also sees bad things.'

The spirit came to house where someone cried. He saw a man there blocking his ears.

'Man,' said the spirit, 'please help me, I want to hear.'

'To hear you need ears,' said the man.

'Can I have yours?' asked the spirit.

'Certainly,' said the man and smiled.

'Oh Father help me,' cried the spirit when he heard a cry, 'what is this sad sound?'

'Walk on through the world,' his father said, 'he who hears also hears bad things.'

Then the spirit saw the most beautiful woman and loved her instantly.

'Beautiful woman, help me,' he said, 'I can think, I can remember, I can feel and I can smell, I can hear, and even see you but still I'm not alive.'

'To live you need life,' said the beautiful woman.

'Can I have yours?' asked the spirit.

'Certainly, because I love you,' said the woman and instantly died.

'Oh Father help me,' cried the man in terrible sorrow when he saw his love was dead.

'Walk on through the world,' his father said, 'they that live also die.'

This kind of story is often found in collections of fairy tales and folk tales (all good sources of other texts for EFL). The repetition is a kind of hook

that helps the teller to remember the tale and the audience to participate in its telling. This same hook is useful to help students remember
language and structure.

Procedure

1 Begin telling this story and as soon as the students recognise the
pattern ask them to tell it to you. Encourage the students' interven-
tion with the question, 'And what do you think happened next?' As the
story develops, the students will need less and less input. They will
take it away from you and you will only need to provide cues.
2 When the story is finished, divide the students into two groups. Ask
one group to tell the story among themselves and to write all the
important verbs in a list. Ask the other group to do the same, this time
writing all the important nouns.
3 Pair off noun-students and verb-students and ask them to make
sentences about the story by matching nouns and verbs. Thus a
noun-student may have written *spirit* and a verb-student *see*. They
may then produce a sentence like, 'The *spirit saw* a beautiful woman'.
Words on the list can be reused. Noun-students do not have to write
down *spirit* once for every time it occurs in the text.
4 Hand out copies of the text for silent reading.

2.15

LEVEL
Lower
intermediate+

FOCUS
Reading for gist,
using link words,
making oral
summaries from
notes

MATERIALS
Class set of a text,
small pieces of
paper

TEXTUAL ITINERARY

Here the emphasis is on how text achieves a sense of coherence through
the words and punctuation that join one statement to another and
which signal whether text is drawing conclusions from what has gone
before, arguing with itself or simply giving further information.

SUGGESTED TEXT
Any, but a prose rich in link words and with long sentences makes the
exercise more successful.

Preparation

1 Construct an itinerary of the text on the board. The itinerary consists
of the important points in each part of each sentence written down in
note form. Link words or punctuation are left out. It should look like a
train map with the important points like stations with a line running
between them. For example, the sentences:

'I always get up at seven and have a shower. Then I have breakfast and go to
work. When I've finished work, I go shopping.'

would give the itinerary:

'get up_____shower_____breakfast_____work_____go shopping'

and the link words:

and, then, and, when.

2 Write each omitted link word on a piece of paper. If sentences have no link words, then write a full stop on the card instead. If you have more students than link words, write some words twice so that you have at least one for every student.

Procedure

1 Give out a copy of the text to each student.
2 Ask the students to read the complete text and sort out any comprehension problems.
3 Tell the students to put away the text. Give out the link words.
4 Ask one student to look at the first part of the itinerary on the board and to try to orally construct a paraphrase of what the text said.
5 Ask the class to think how they will link the first part of the itinerary to the second. Ask for a suitable link word or for a full stop if it fits. The student who thinks they have a link word says it and tries to reconstruct what follows. Ask the class if the link word can join these phrases or not. Intervene when the class is wrong. If the link fails, then ask another student to try with their word. If the paraphrase is acceptable, ask a third student to say the complete sentence with the link.
6 Continue until the class has gone through the whole itinerary.
7 Suggest that students use the itinerary to write summaries of the text or to practise making rapid oral summaries to each other in pairs.

TALK BACK

Through text, writers talk to readers and to themselves, answering their queries, dismissing their objections or giving them the information they need. This activity seeks to expose the hidden conversation and turn any text into a script that students can perform. The preparation may sound elaborate but can actually take the form of hurried notes on scrap paper that are later transferred to the board.

SUGGESTED TEXT
Any text that is not written in dialogue form. Good for ESP texts.

Preparation

1 Read your text as if it were arguing with you, answering your questions, dealing with your objections, dismissing your fears and inciting your comment. Imagine that the text was being 'told to you' and that you had to join in the conversation to get your speaker to talk it out. If you are talking back to an opinionated text, you could state what it is arguing against. If you have a narrative, you could talk

2.16

LEVEL
Elementary+

FOCUS
Reading for detailed understanding, analysis of textual arguments, reading out loud

MATERIALS
Class set of a text

about the characters as if they were mutual acquaintances, comment on what is said and try to get the speaker to continue the story. Sometimes you will just write questions but at an elementary level even this can be interesting.

2 Write what you would say in order to get the substance of the text told to you sentence by sentence, so converting it into a dialogue.

3 Write the parts of this 'dialogue frame' in scrambled order on the board.

Procedure

1 Hand out a copy of the text to each student.

2 Put the students into pairs and ask each pair to write down the parts of the dialogue frame on the board in the order in which they fit the text. They should work on one piece of paper. For example, a class of lower-intermediate students may read this text:

She followed him everywhere. Once she found him on some island in the middle of the Atlantic where the people wore 19th Century clothes and spoke a lost dialect of English. She found him riding up a street on a great black horse. He touched his hat, smiled and rode by. But she found out where he lived and waited till he took her in.

© Longman Group UK Ltd 1991

The dialogue frame on the board might be:

Oh yes, I think I've heard of that place. Did she go all that way?
She was crazy. A man like that isn't worth it.
He must have looked a sight.
So he used to leave her?
You mean he didn't even talk to her. What did she do? Take the next boat out?
I suppose he expected her to follow.

The students might write:

So he used to leave her?
I suppose he expected her to follow?
Oh yes, I think I've heard of that place. Did she go all that way?
He must have looked a sight.
You mean he didn't even talk to her? What did she do? Take the next boat out?
She was crazy. A man like that isn't worth it!

3 Ask one student in the pair to read the dialogue frame and the other to talk back by using the text. They should try to do more than simply read the text. They should make it sound like a genuine conversation. This can be very difficult but the right tone of voice and the insertion of a few exclamations can help a lot. The students should realise that more than one version may be possible. The correct answer is a dialogue that sounds good. From the above text and frame you might get this dialogue:

Student 1	So he used to leave her?
Student 2	Yes, she followed him everywhere.
Student 1	I suppose he expected her to follow?
Student 2	I don't know. But once she found him on that island in the middle of the Atlantic where the people wore old-fashioned clothes and spoke in a lost dialect of English.
Student 1	Oh yes, I think I've heard of that place. Did she go all that way?
Student 2	Yes she did. She found him riding up a street on a great black horse.
Student 1	He must have looked a sight!
Student 2	And you know he just touched his hat, smiled and rode by.
Student 1	You mean he didn't even talk to her! What did she do? Take the next boat out?
Student 2	No, she found where he lived and waited till he took her in.
Student 1	She was crazy. A man like that isn't worth it!

4 Get the pairs to practise their dialogues.

5 Ask each pair to swap their ordered dialogue frames with another pair.

6 Take back the texts.

7 Ask the students to practise the dialogues using someone else's frame and without the help of the text. One partner reads the prompts from the frame and the other improvises using the ideas in the text.

8 Select some pairs to perform their dialogues in front of the class. The result can sometimes be disjointed and hilarious, so a good supportive atmosphere is necessary.

VARIATION

When the students are familiar with the idea of a dialogue frame, they can write their own. Use two texts or one divided text and two groups. Each group writes a frame for the other to try to fit on the text.

PUNCTUATION LESSON

A writer not only makes text cohere through the logic of its argument and the way its words refer back and forth to each other but also through the basic device of punctuation. This activity serves as a reminder to students that in order to punctuate a text correctly you must first have some understanding of it.

Preparation

1 Produce a version of the text that has no punctuation and make one copy per student.

2 List the different kinds of punctuation used in your text. If your class is elementary then only list the full stops.

2.17

LEVEL
Elementary+

FOCUS
Reading for gist, punctuating text, using English punctuation words, reading out loud

MATERIALS
Class set of any texts

Procedure

1 Teach or revise all the words for the punctuation used by your text.
2 Take any text that you are not using for this exercise and dictate the punctuation but not the words. For example, this text:

'The moon, the trees, the mountains,' he said slowly, 'all this can be yours!'

is read, with as much expression as if you were reading words, as:

open inverted commas comma comma comma close inverted commas comma open inverted commas exclamation mark close inverted commas

The student writes:

" , , ," "!"

3 Assign one punctuation sentence to each student and ask them to write a sentence that fits the punctuation.
4 Get each student to read out their sentence and the punctuation as if they were dictating it. For example:

Open inverted commas I eat comma I sleep comma I talk to the wall comma I don't go and see people comma close inverted commas, etc.

5 Put the students into pairs and give one copy of the text without punctuation to each pair. Ask each pair to punctuate the text.
6 Ask one student to read their punctuated text out loud. This student should not read out the punctuation. Instead the class should shout out the punctuation whenever the student comes to it, thus interrupting their reading of the text.

2.18

LEVEL
Intermediate+

FOCUS
Discussing a writer's intentions, orally reconstructing a text

MATERIALS
Class set of any text

INVENTING FUNCTIONS

This activity shifts the focus away from how sentences lock together to make text, towards the consideration of what each sentence is really trying to achieve.

The functional description of language is popular with many language teachers because it seems to break language into series of purposeful and teachable units. Among linguists the idea has lost much ground, partly because it is very difficult to determine what the communicative intention of any given statement is. However, this activity analyses just that intention. The attempt to determine a writer's communicative intention in any given sentence can stimulate interesting discussion and also make a student more sensitive to a writer's purposes.

Preparation

Study the text and decide whether you can give clear functional labels to every sentence in the text. Do not worry about being too exact or always using the correct terms. Just ask yourself what the writer is trying to do in a particular sentence. Assert a fact? Describe a feeling? Or what? For example, the following text could give the functions listed below it:

Christopher felt his jaw drop. Not a second before – that very second! – he had made up his mind to ask Valentine Wannop to become his mistress that night. It was no good any more he said to himself. She loved him, he knew, with a deep, an unshakable passion, just as his passion was a devouring element that covered his whole mind as the atmosphere envelopes the earth. Were they, then, to go down to death separated by years, with no word ever spoken? To what end? For whose benefit? The whole world conspired to force them together. To resist became weariness.

Ford Madox Ford, *Parade's End*, Penguin 1982 p214

Functions

1 describing feelings/expressing understanding
2 describing a past thought
3 describing a realisation
4 describing feelings
5 speculating
6 wondering/rejecting an idea
7 wondering/rejecting an idea
8 describing a feeling or accepting a circumstance
9 submitting

Procedure

1 Explain to the class that you are going to think about why people say or write particular things. They should consider what writers are trying to do with a particular sentence. You can illustrate this in the following way:

Teacher	If I say 'I'm sorry', What am I doing? Showing anger?
Student	You're saying sorry
Teacher	Saying sorry?
Student	Apologising

Try to get students to think beyond the obvious.

Teacher	Apologising yes, but why?
Student	To teach about apologising
Teacher	Giving an example?
Student	Yes, giving an example
Teacher	So, apologising and exemplifying

2 Give more examples and modify the students' suggestions less and less. Make them feel confident about their own terms. These ideas can be difficult and take time to put across.

3 Put the students into pairs and give each student a copy of the text. Ask each pair to go through the text and to state the communicative intention of each sentence. Remind the class that this is not a 'right or wrong' exercise. Circulate and help them to develop expressive functional labels.

4 Ask students to tell you how they have described each sentence. Discuss differences of opinion. Write down the function name or names that you and the class prefer on the board until you have a complete list.

5 Put away the text and use the list of functions to get the class to orally reconstruct the text. Students should not aim to follow the wording of the text exactly but you can help by supplying some vocabulary when needed.

6 In pairs, the students imagine they are going to write a short paragraph about any subject raised by the text.

7 Each pair writes down the functions they will use in their paragraph.

8 Invite one student to the board and ask them to write down their title then the functions that they will use.

9 The rest of the class try to supply the text orally.

2.19

LEVEL
Lower
intermediate+

FOCUS
Parsing text, orally
constructing text

MATERIALS
Class set of any
text

PARTS OF SPEECH PEOPLE

The emphasis here is on the grammatical structure of sentences. The purpose of the activity is threefold: the achievement of some understanding of how a text is constructed at sentence level, grammar awareness, and invented but structured oral expression. The activity was devised for ESL classes in secondary schools but is useful for ESP and general English classes.

Preparation

Divide the text into two and prepare one half text per student and one complete text per student.

Procedure

1 Check that the class understands the basic parts of speech: adjective, verb, noun.

2 Divide the class into two teams. Hand out copies of one half of the text to Team 1 and of the other half to Team 2.

3 Ask each team to produce a version of the text which has no nouns, verbs or adjectives in it. Instead of the word itself they write the part of speech. Pronouns should be treated as nouns and auxiliary verbs

or verbs before verbs should be left in the text. For example, the sentence:

Alison went to stay at a large house in the country.

would be written as:

N went to V at a Adj N in the N.

Students should leave structure clues, such as:

The man looking at my friend.
The N V*ing* at my N

They should remember that V*ed* could signify an irregular past.

4   Each team writes its new version of the text on the board.
5   Divide each team into three groups: 'nouns', 'adjectives' and 'verbs'. Each group makes a list of various examples of their particular part of speech. So the noun group makes a list of nouns, the verb group a list of verbs, etc.
6   Team 2 look at the Team 1 version of the text on the board. If the first missing word is a noun then ask a member of the noun group to suggest a noun, if it's a verb then ask the verb group to suggest a verb and so on. Do the same for each missing item in the sentence but insist that the words used must create a sentence that makes sense. Students will already have an idea about the subject matter of the text from their own half. Try to get them to make sentences that express this content but do not force the point if they get stuck. Repeat with the next sentence and so on until all of the first half of the text has been rewritten. For the example sentence,

N went to V at a Adj N in the N

the students might come up with the following words:

Noun group	John
Verb group	eat
Adj. group	large
Noun group	restaurant
Noun group	city

These words make the sentence

John went to eat at a large restaurant in the city.

When Team 2 has completed Team 1's text, Team 1 does the same with Team 2's text.

7   Students from Team 1 form pairs with students from Team 2.
8   The partner from Team 2 reads the first sentence from the altered text on the board. The partner from Team 1 corrects by reading the original sentence and so on until they have completed their section of the text. They change roles for the second half of the text.

2.20

LEVEL
Intermediate+

FOCUS
Reading for gist, discussing the relationships between words

MATERIALS
Class set of any text

WORD RELATIONS

The interest here is in the words and phrases that are most important to a text's argument. These words are treated like the points on a map that the student must link together in order to recreate the text.

Procedure

1 Hand out one copy of the text to each student. They read the text in order to find words which they consider important to its overall meaning, powerful in their effect on them, or difficult and obscure. They underline these words.
2 After the reading, the students call out their words. Write them on the board in a random fashion, sorting out any problems of meaning.
3 One student comes to the board and draws a line between two words whose sense appears related in some way. This relatedness can have any basis but the student must justify it to the class after the line is drawn. Other students repeat until the board resembles a route map joining all the words to each other. (Even words with the most distant meaning can be made to relate in some way.)
4 In pairs, students follow the map, discussing the relationship between the words and also recalling the text as they do so.

2.21

LEVEL
Elementary+

FOCUS
Oral and written reproduction of text, appreciating the construction of text

MATERIALS
Class set of any short text, OHP and transparencies (optional)

DESTROYING THE TEXT

Here students work more at the level of individual words than sentences. The object is to get students to pull words from a text and to put them into another context. The text then falls apart and the students must relocate the words in order to rebuild it.

Preparation

1 Make one copy of a text for each student.
2 Write the text on the board or photocopy it onto an OHP transparency. If you are using an OHP, you will also need to have another spare transparency.

Procedure

1 Hand out one copy of the text to each student.
2 Ask students to read the text and to tell you any words that they do not understand. Write the words on the board and elicit the meanings from the class or explain them yourself.
3 Divide the class into pairs.

4 Tell the pairs to write new sentences from the words in the text. The sentences can be about anything but they must make sense. The only other rule is that they cannot put words together in their sentence if they are together in the text. However, if you have two words together, *the* and *farmer*, for example, and they can find a *the* anywhere else in the text then the combination *the farmer* is allowed. Tell them to treat the text as a bank of jumbled words that they must turn into sentences. Advise them to try to use the more difficult words that you have listed on the board.

5 Allow the students only a little time because they will probably have to change their sentences during the next stage of the exercise.

6 Project the text or display it on the board.

7 Ask a student to come forward and write their first sentence on the board. If the sentence is correct rub out all the words from the text that are used by it and replace them with '_____'.

8 Invite someone else to make another sentence with the words that are left.

9 Continue until no more sentences can be made.

10 Work round the class, asking the students to orally build up the text again by using the words in their sentences. Here is a text I have used with elementary students:

Another Mouth to Feed

The old man was very rich. He thought:
'I am too rich to enter heaven.'
He gave his fine cars to the poor. He thought:
'I am still too rich to enter heaven.' He made his house into a hospital and went away. He thought:
'I cannot live more than five years.' He counted out five gold pieces, and gave all his other money to the poor.
One night he woke up frightened. He thought:
'If I die tonight, I will still be too rich. I will have five gold pieces.' So he found a beggar and gave them all to him.
The next day he saw a poor farmer.
'Oh no,' the old man panicked, 'I have nothing to give him.' Then he had an idea.'I know', he cried, 'I will give the farmer my last possession, myself.'
'What do I want that for?' said the farmer. 'You're just another mouth to feed.'

© Longman Group UK Ltd 1991

In a recent teacher training session the group gave this about half way through:

The —— man —— very rich. He thought:
'I am too rich to enter heaven.'
He —— his fine cars —— the poor. He thought:
'— am still too rich to enter ———.' —— made his —— into a ———
— and —— away. He thought:
'I cannot live more than five years.' He counted out five —— pieces, and

gave all his other money to —— poor.
One night he ——— up ————. He thought:
'If I die tonight, I will still be too rich. —— will have —— gold pieces.' So
he —— a beggar —— gave them all to him.
The next day he saw a poor ——.
'Oh no,' —— old man ———, 'I have nothing to give him.' Then he had
an idea.'—— know', he cried, 'I will give —— farmer —— last ———,
myself.'
'What do I want that for?' said the   ——. 'You're just another mouth to – –
—.'

The house was five years old
The farmer panicked and woke frightened
I gave gold to heaven
I feed the farmer
I found my possession
He went to hospital

2.22

LEVEL
Elementary+

FOCUS
Reading out loud,
listening to text,
understanding
sentence structure

MATERIALS
Class set of any
text

WORDS THAT DON'T FIT

An understanding of a text can be conveyed by a linking of words crucial to the overall meaning but it can also be shown by the search for and identification of terms that are not necessary. In this activity the inserted words relate closely to the theme of the text, so their exclusion requires more than a cursory scanning of text. The insertions are also made by the students themselves and since they must be nonsensical they demand an initial awareness of sense.

Preparation

1 Decide on a title for the text and count the number of sentences. If some of the sentences are very long and can be easily divided, consider them as two.
2 Divide the text into two equal halves.

Procedure

1 Divide the class into pairs and tell them the title of the text and the number of sentences in it.
2 Ask each pair to think of words which they associate with the title. They should try to think of as many words as there are sentences in the text and write them in a list. If they have problems thinking of enough words, help out with some of your own or allow shorter lists. When they have enough words, tell them to tear the list in half. Each partner keeps one half of the list.

3 Give each student one half of the text.

4 Students now insert into the text the words they have on their part of the list. They must write one word into every sentence. The only conditions are that the words must be placed so that they do not make sense, and that identical words cannot be placed together. Of course, sophisticated students can go for interesting effects so that the insertions almost sound meaningful. This adds to the interest of the exercise.

5 Each student finds a new partner.

6 Students read the text with the inserted words to each other. The student listening should not see the text. When the listener hears an inserted word, they ask the reader to pause long enough to let them write it down.

7 In pairs, students check whether their lists of inserted words are correct. Ask some to read their lists to the class. Encourage the class to ask individuals why they wrote the words they did and what they expected the text to be about.

PRETEACHER

The question of whether to preteach vocabulary has never been an easy one to answer. One advantage is that the student who has mastered difficult words before they approach the text can concentrate on the content and theme without having their mind cluttered with too many linguistic problems. One disadvantage is that the preteaching session can become an overextended vocabulary lesson where words are taught out of context and the text itself is forgotten.

This simple activity tries to make a virtue out of the lack of a context by insisting that words are taught entirely through examples that are different from the text while giving the preteaching task to the students themselves so that it does not degenerate into an 'I teach and you listen' session.

Preparation

Divide the texts into two roughly equal halves.

Procedure

1 Divide the class into two groups.

2 Hand out the first half of the text to Group 1 and the second half to Group 2.

3 Ask each group to scan their half of the text and make a list of all the words they do not understand. They should only make one list per group but it should include words that are understood by one person but not by others.

2.23

LEVEL
Elementary+

FOCUS
Using dictionaries, explaining the meanings of words, rapid reading

MATERIALS
Class set of any text, monolingual dictionaries

4 Give out the dictionaries and ask Group 1 to exchange word lists with Group 2.

5 Ask each group to divide up the words as equally as possible among themselves. If there are fewer words than students, then some words must be given to a pair of students.

6 Tell the students to teach their assigned word to the class in turn. They can do this with examples, illustrations, explanations or mime. Translation is not allowed. The word cannot be taught through the text as the other students will not generally have read the part where it appears. The exercise is more fun if students are actually encouraged to role play you or other teachers.

7 After the preteaching phase students read the text silently to themselves.

2.24

LEVEL
Elementary+

FOCUS
Using dictionaries, rapid reading, discussing procedures

MATERIALS
Class set of any text, bi- or monolingual dictionaries

DICTIONARY GAME 1
THE WORD RACE

This activity encourages students to scan texts for unfamiliar vocabulary and to use dictionaries quickly and efficiently.

Preparation

Count the number of words in the text which you think are likely to cause problems and time your own reading of the text.

Procedure

1 Hand out the texts and dictionaries.

2 Divide the class into two teams.

3 Tell the students that each team has a limited time to read the text, find as many unknown words as they can and look them up in the dictionary.

4 Each team has one minute to decide how they will approach the task. When the time is up, they begin.

5 When the allotted time has elapsed, ask a member of Team 1 to say any word from the text. Someone from Team 2 must give two examples of how the word is used. The first example shows how the word is used in the text (either through a reading of the relevant sentence or a paraphrase). A second example explains the word's meaning in another context. For example, from an ESP sample text about the four stroke cycle the word chosen might be *intake*:
The examples given could be:
- The *intake* stroke – the piston draws in the petrol to the cylinder.
- Breathing is an *intake* of air.

The teams score one mark for one correct answer, two marks for two. If the answer is incorrect, then the other team must answer their own question for one mark. The question stage ends when all the difficult words have been dealt with.

EXTENSION

1 Take the texts back then write all the words that have caused difficulties on the board in their order of appearance in the text.
2 Invite one student to the board and ask them to choose a word, then write a sentence giving a context for the word. The sentence should relate to something that is said in the text.
3 Continue until you have a sentence for each word.
4 Students think very hard for a few minutes about what, if anything, they would write between the sentences in order to connect them. They need not say anything.
5 Students read the text again in order to find out how well they have mentally reconstructed it.

DICTIONARY GAME 2
THE SNAKE PIT

This activity tries to train students to use dictionaries quickly and efficiently. The activity uses a short adventure game sequence or 'parallel text' which means that a successful reading of the main text results in the successful negotiation of another text. The parallel text concerns making an escape from a snake pit. As students pass along the route, they leave difficult words attached to its different stages. They thus construct a kind of mnemonic map where words are made memorable by being attached to particular places or events.

Preparation

Draw the example adventure map on the board or make up one of your own. (See page 67.)

Procedure

1 Divide the class into two teams.
2 Ask someone from Team 1 to read the first sentence of the text out loud.
3 Ask someone from Team 2 to question Team 1 about any word in the sentence. If their answer is right, tell them they move up the ladder to the first level. If their answer is wrong, tell them they are falling back into the pit of snakes but they have one hope – the Great Book of

2.25

LEVEL
Elementary+

FOCUS
Using dictionaries, reading out loud, rapid reading

MATERIALS
Class set of any text, bi- or monolingual dictionaries, a stopwatch

Words! Give them a dictionary and tell them to put themselves right. Give them thirty seconds (more or less according to the ability of the class) to find the word. The meaning they give must fit the use of the word in the text. While they are searching, you can pile on the pressure with a commentary! Tell them the snakes are crawling up the ladder and going to pull them down, or whatever terrible scenario you fancy! Even get Team 2 to join in. If Team 1 cannot find the word or cannot answer correctly in the time, then they stay at the bottom level and begin with the first sentence again at their next turn.

4 Write the problem word onto the first stairway of the map.

5 Ask a student from Team 2 to read the first sentence of the text. Get Team 1 to ask them a question about any word in that sentence. If Team 2 answer successfully or find their word in the dictionary, then they climb to the first level and read the second sentence. If they are successful again, they climb to the second level. Then it is the turn of Team 1 again.

6 When a team are not successful, they either fall a level or are delayed in some way. The delay continues until they give a good answer. The question about the problem sentence can change each time so a bad predicament can get worse. Always write the problem word on the map. With the map opposite, the game would go as follows:

1 Good answer = Climb the ladder
   Bad answer   = Fall into the snake pit

2 Good answer = See the well and go up the stairs
   Bad answer   = Fall into the well

3 Good answer = Cross the bridge and climb the stairs
   Bad answer   = Cross the bridge and fall in the pond

4 Good answer = Step over the dragon and go up
   Bad answer   = Wake the dragon and get chased into a cage

5 Good answer = Cross the lake before it burns
   Bad answer   = The lake burns and you swim to the island of ice

6 Good answer = Walk past the tree
   Bad answer   = Eat the fruit and sleep

7 Good answer = Walk through the garden
   Bad answer   = You like it, stay and cannot leave

8 Good answer = Get to the surface
   Bad answer   = Work in the mine

9 Good answer = The gate shuts after you go through
   Bad answer   = The gate shuts before you go through

10 Good answer = Get to the cliff before the dogs
    Bad answer   = The dogs chase you up a tree

11 Good answer = Get down the cliff and home
    Bad answer   = The rope breaks and you die

© Longman Group UK Ltd

7 If the text is not finished when students reach the end of this map, you can extend the journey through more stages or demoralise everybody by making them start at the bottom again.

8 Ask each team to recount their journey, saying what happened to them while recalling the meanings of the words that they were asked about.

VARIATION

When students are familiar with this activity, each team can devise an adventure map for the other.

2.26

LEVEL
Lower
intermediate+

FOCUS
Deducing word
meanings from
context, defining
words

MATERIALS
Class set of a text,
monolingual
dictionaries

TEXTUAL BLUFF

I have never been able to make the radio and television game of *Call My Bluff* work as a vocabulary teaching activity in class. This may be because it is too much of a British institution to be immediately comprehensible to foreigners. Also, students probably need to have seen the game played in order to fully understand how it operates. Finally, the necessary stratagems of bluff and invention may run ahead of the language of all but the most advanced level. However, a textual frame can bring the activity down to earth and make it more relevant. When the real and unreal definition must fit a context, the game loses some of its psychological subtlety but gains as an activity for practising defining and for teaching new vocabulary.

SUGGESTED TEXT
Any with a good quantity of unfamiliar vocabulary.

Preparation

Underline the words in the text that you think will cause problems to the students and divide the underlined text into two parts with an equal number of underlined words in each part.

Procedure

1 Give out the text halves and divide the class into two teams. One team will work with one half of the text and the other with the other half.
2 Ask each team to look up the meanings of the underlined words in their part of the text.
3 Ask each team to think of two untrue definitions for each word. These definitions must make sense in terms of the context. You may have to help in order to get the definitions sounding authentic and also by demonstrating what you mean at the beginning. For example, for the sentence: *he put up his friends for a few days* they could offer the following alternative definitions:

   a Put up = to entertain or to amuse.
   b Put up = to give a bed to, to give somewhere to sleep to.
   c Put up = to endure or bear as in 'he didn't like his friends but he put them up.'

4 Ask Team 1 to present three definitions of one word, one correct according to the dictionary and two false. Team 2 consult the text and each other to decide which definition is correct. If Team 2 choose correctly, they score one point. Team 1 continues until they have covered their part of the text.
5 Team 2 do the same with the words in their part of the text. Continue until all the words in this second part have been defined.
6 Get students from Team 2 to read Team 1's part of the text round the class. Ask each reader about the meaning of the underlined words they come to.

7 Continue with Team 1 reading Team 2's part of the text.

ACKNOWLEDGEMENT
Call My Bluff was proposed as a vocabulary teaching technique in *Vocabulary* (Morgan and Rinvolucri 1986).

CLOZE CHARADES

The emphasis here is on the sounds from which a word is built and on the meaning given to it by a context. The gap-finder cloze that is used here is, in my view, better than the normal cloze because it challenges the student on two levels. The student must have a feel for the language in order to spot where a word is needed then an accurate sense of structure in order to know what to insert.

Preparation

1 Prepare the text to make the kind of gap-finder cloze test shown on page 70. In this cloze the places where words are missing are not indicated. One word in every line has been removed from the text. The student must find where the word is missing, decide what that word should be and write it in the space provided at the end of the line. The words that you want to omit depend on your language teaching point. In this activity you do not have to be certain that the students will know the word that has been left out, or even a good substitute for it. In fact, it can often be entertaining for everyone if they do not!
2 Divide the prepared text in two.
3 Write down a list of the omitted words and cut it into two.

Procedure

1 Divide the class into pairs.
2 Give each partner a different half of the prepared text and the half of the word list that does not match that part of the text.
3 Tell the students that there is a word missing from each line of the text and that they must mark where this is and write the word at the end of the line.

2.27

LEVEL
Elementary+

FOCUS
Reading comprehension, mime and constructing text

MATERIALS
Class set of any text

Gap-finder cloze test

The Guarantee of Peace

Part One
The sun warmed Fred when he/the huge ————— *entered* —————
square. There was a crowd balloons. ——————————————
They were going to fun. The balloons ——————————————
had writing them. But he couldn't ——————————————
quite their message. ——————————————
A little later a of people began ——————————————
to, 'freedom.' At first no one ——————————————
noticed. The cheered and seemed ——————————————
to bigger. He shouted 'freedom' ——————————————
because seemed the right thing to ——————————————
say. Two men began carry him away. ——————————————
They put him in a with lots of ——————————————
other people. They took him the ——————————————
'state security' office so felt ——————————————
safe. There was a young girl to him, ——————————————
and she could not screaming. ——————————————

Part Two
They fell out of the when the doors ——————————————
opened and Fred laughed but the were ——————————————
crying with fear. They all to ——————————————
stand in the yard an hour. At ——————————————
last they led him into office. ——————————————
'Fred,' the man in uniform, looking ——————————————
at his identity card. Fred not like the ——————————————
photo there, it not like him at all. ——————————————
'Yes that is me,' Fred him. ——————————————
'Ah Fred,' the policeman. 'We ——————————————
have to keep the peace, you that, ——————————————
don't you?' Fred like the good ——————————————
citizen he always been. ——————————————
'That's we have to guarantee ——————————————
your peace, forever. You my meaning.' ——————————————
And Fred like ash tapped off his cigarette. ——————————————.

Part One		*Part Two*	
entered	get	van	told
with	that	others	said
have	to	had	know
on	van	for	agreed
read	to	an	had
lot	he	said	why
shout	next	did	get
crowd	stop	was	felt

4 Tell the students that if they cannot find the location of the missing word or decide on a word that fits, they can ask their partner to help.

5 The partner cannot help by saying the word, but must instead mime it. The partner can mime it by first showing the number of syllables with their fingers. Next, they may try to mime each syllable separately. They could do this by miming words that sound the same as the syllables. For example, if the word is *particle* they might mime *part* by dividing a piece of paper into *parts* then *tickle* by *tickling* their partner. Then they gesture to show that the words must be put together as *part-tickle* and said quickly to give *particle*. For lower intermediate or elementary texts most words will probably be of one or two syllables. They will often be the kind of word that can be mimed as a single unit.

Articulating, writing or mouthing of words is not allowed. The students trying to find the word will speak their approximations and their partners will use gesture to show how close or far away these are. Students should speak fairly quietly however, as they may help rival partnerships to complete the text if they are overheard. For this activity, only the words that are actually in the text can be counted as correct, even though others may fit. Words which do fit but which are not used by the writer can be written against the line as possible alternatives and discussed with the teacher afterwards.

6 Students swap roles when the first part of the text is finished.

7 The first pair to complete all the text correctly wins.

THINKING METAPHORICALLY 1
MATCHING THE METAPHOR

2.28

LEVEL
Intermediate+

FOCUS
Making up metaphors, matching words and metaphors, thinking about style.

MATERIALS
Class set of a text

The emphasis here is on the use of words in an important area that is often neglected by ELT teachers – that of metaphor. Even supposedly literal styles contain a great deal more metaphor than one might think. Scientists use metaphor to describe the universe. Metaphor is fundamental to oral and written communication. The term may also be crucial to the way we remember and to the way we think.

The first part of the activity could also stand alone and as a creative drill for practising the structures that signal metaphors (*like, as...as,* etc), building vocabulary and encouraging creativity. However, these activities as a whole were developed for ESL students whose level was one where the line between ESL and mother tongue teaching becomes blurred and the ESL teacher starts to wonder if they are not just doing what could be done in ordinary English classes. Therefore mother tongue teachers might also find this activity useful, as might trainers who want to raise language awareness in teacher training sessions.

SUGGESTED TEXT

A short text with a metaphorical style. Creative writing works best. Some scientific texts benefit from this treatment, particularly those dealing with difficult and abstract theories of cosmology or quantum physics.

Preparation

Locate the metaphors in the text. For each, in order, write down the literal expression with the same meaning. Make a copy of the list of literal expressions for each student.

Procedure

1 Give each student a copy of the list of literal expressions.
2 Get the students into pairs.
3 Ask each pair to make metaphors for the items on the list.
4 Students continue until they have made up metaphors for all the items on the list, then they change partners.
5 In their new pairs one partner reads out a metaphor from their list and the other matches it with what they think is an appropriate item by making a sentence. The discussion might be as follows.

Student 1   A small train station
Student 2   The lift was like a small train station
Student 1   No, the reception desk was like a small train station.

6 When each pair has finished their list, read the first item to the class and ask students to offer their preferred metaphors. The class decide which one they like best.
7 Begin to write the full text on the board. Ask the class to help you rewrite it by substituting their metaphors for the original ones.
8 Hand out a copy of the original text to each student.
9 Ask the students to compare the original text with the new one on the board, discussing which they prefer and why, and how the new version is true or untrue to the writer's intentions.

VARIATION

Prepare a version of the text without metaphors and underline the words that the original text treated metaphorically. Hand out this version of the text instead of the list of words then proceed as from Step 3.

THINKING METAPHORICALLY 2
STUDENTS' SEARCH

LEVEL
Intermediate+

This activity is concerned with metaphors in texts. Students should be familiar with the idea of metaphor for this to work well. It may be useful to do Activity 2.28 *Matching the metaphor* before attempting this one.

FOCUS
Making up metaphors, matching words and metaphors, thinking about style

SUGGESTED TEXT

A text with a metaphorical style. Creative writing works best. Some scientific texts benefit from this treatment, particularly those dealing with difficult and abstract theories of cosmology or quantum physics.

MATERIALS
Class set of a text

Preparation

Divide the text in two.

Procedure

1 Divide the class into two groups. Give a copy of the first half of the text to each student in Group 1, and a copy of the second half to each student in Group 2.
2 Collectively the groups identify the literal items that are treated metaphorically in their text and make a list of these literal items.
3 Once they have completed the list and each made their own copy, every student from Group 1 finds a partner from Group 2.
4 The students in each pair swap their lists of literal expressions. Both students independently write metaphors for each of the literal items on their partner's list and keep it.
5 The two groups then reform, and collectively choose their favourite metaphors from the lists they have in front of them.
6 Ask one Group 1 student to join Group 2, and one Group 2 student to join Group 1. These two students tell their adoptive group what happens in the part of the text they have read, in the simplest and most literal way, excluding all metaphor.
7 Group 1 then collectively writes out the second part of the text (working from the Group 2 student's spoken description of the text), including the favourite metaphors chosen earlier. Likewise, Group 2 writes out the first part of the text, using their favourite metaphors.
8 Hand out the complete text.
9 Ask students to compare the original text with the one they have made, discussing which they prefer and why, then how their own version is true or untrue to the writer's intentions.

2.30

LEVEL
Intermediate+

FOCUS
Finding meanings
for metaphors,
matching
meanings and
metaphors,
thinking about
style

MATERIALS
Class set of a text

THINKING METAPHORICALLY 3
METAPHORS LOOKING FOR A MEANING

In this activity metaphors are 'set adrift' from the text and the students must attach them to a meaning.

SUGGESTED TEXT

A text with a metaphorical style. Creative writing works best. Some scientific texts benefit from this treatment, particularly those dealing with difficult and abstract theories of cosmology or quantum physics.

Preparation

Prepare a list of the metaphorical expressions in the text and write it on the board. This text could be used for advanced students:

Out, out brief candle!
Life's but a walking shadow, a poor player
That struts and frets his hour upon the stage,
And then is heard no more; it is a tale
Told by an idiot, full of sound and fury,
Signifying nothing.

William Shakespeare, *Macbeth*, Act V, Scene V.

It would give the following list:

brief candle
a walking shadow
a poor player that struts and frets his hour upon the stage and then is heard no more.
a tale told by an idiot, full of sound and fury, but signifying nothing.

Procedure

1 Check that all vocabulary is understood.
2 Rub the list off the board. Tell the students that you are going to read them these 'detached metaphors' one by one. Ask them to listen, then to let the metaphor channel their thoughts so that they follow a chain of associations.
3 Ask the students to relax and close their eyes. Read the first metaphor. Ask students to think: 'What do you see?' 'What do you hear?' 'What do you smell?' 'How do you feel?' Allow students time to follow their thoughts. Repeat with the other metaphors, gradually phasing out the questions. Allow time for thoughts to develop.
4 When you have finished, ask a student to try to describe the picture they have built up around the first metaphor. Tell the class that this is a picture with a meaning. Ask what it means. Try to narrow this meaning down to something simple. With the sample text from

Macbeth you would just be aiming for *life* in every case, but don't force it. Your conversation may be something like this:

Student 1	I saw a candle burning in a room. I heard someone breathing.
Teacher	They were asleep?
Student 1	Yes, asleep.
Teacher	And you smelt?
Student 1	The candle.
Teacher	Wax burning?
Student 1	Yes.
Teacher	And you felt?
Student 1	Sad.
Teacher	Why?
Student 1	Time was going.
Teacher	So your picture was about time going?
Student 1	Yes, I think so.

5 When you have asked one student about each metaphor, do an association exercise. Say the first metaphor, touch the student next to you, ask them to say the first word they think of, then ask the next student to say whatever comes into their head, and so on round the class.

6 Give students the text. Ask them to read it in order to find out if the metaphors actually describe the sort of things they had thought of.

CHAPTER 3

Headlines and titles

Titles and headlines often sum up the content of a text. They are written in order to attract the reader's attention or even to tell them whether they need to spend time reading a particular text. The reader therefore naturally predicts the content of a text from its title. Even a cryptic title or headline gives rise to an internal dialogue about what will follow or incites a curiosity that asks to be satisfied. Working in the other direction, the students who can write a good title or a headline for a piece will express their understanding of its essential meaning. The search for a good title can set up a debate that draws out all the important points of a text.

What follows are ways to formulate these themes and create the foundations of successful text-based lessons.

3.1

LEVEL
Intermediate+

FOCUS
Reading for gist, giving and listening to oral summaries, matching texts and titles

MATERIALS
Newspaper articles, bi- or monolingual dictionaries

MATCHING THE HEADLINE TO THE STORY

A new version of a classic exercise to help students read for a main idea, explain that idea to the class and set up a forum for discussion. The system here attaches words to titles and so will both preteach troublesome vocabulary and encourage prediction of the content of a text at one go.

SUGGESTED TEXTS
At least six short newspaper articles or 'letters to the Editor' complete with headlines. Enough copies to give one article to each student. A good supply of monolingual or bilingual dictionaries.

Preparation

1 Separate the headlines from the articles. Number the headlines.
2 Divide the board, vertically, into one wide column and one narrow column.

Procedure

1 Give each student a headline and an article that does not belong to the headline.
2 Ask each student to read their article. When they come to a word they do not know, ask them to write it on a piece of paper then to copy the phrase it comes from on the board with a blank where the word should be. The phrase should make complete sense and should be written in the wide column. They can copy the whole

sentence if it is short. The problem phrases should only be written up once.

3 While the students are doing this, walk round the class and write the words that you see on their papers into the other column on the board. These words should be in random order. Take the papers in when they have finished to make sure that you have written all the words on the board.

4 When the students have finished, ask them to look up the meanings of the words in the narrow column that they do not know. They should do this individually. Then ask them to see if they can fit the words into the sentences on the other side of the board. This should be a mental exercise only. They should not write anything.

5 Ask three or four students with different headlines to come to the board and claim any sentences which they think belong to their headline. They do this by writing their headline number over the blanks in the sentences. The same sentence may be claimed by several headlines at once. No one should say anything.

6 Each student reads their headline out loud. Repeat until every student has heard every other headline. Use this for pronunciation practice.

7 Ask one student to explain the content of their article to the group. The students who think they have the headline of this article should not say so. The rest of the group must try to identify the holder of the appropriate headline.

8 Ask the student with the headline to go to the board and renumber any phrase which they now think does or does not belong to their headline. The student who has the article can help if necessary.

9 Repeat with each of the articles.

10 Ask the class to tell you how to fill in the blanks. Act dumb and do exactly what they say. Let them argue about it. Correct if necessary at the end.

11 Rub out the phrases. Leave only the word that was inserted in the blank with its number over it.

12 Ask a student to read the first headline. Look for a word marked 1 and try to elicit a context for the word. You can use this to build up the article again. Repeat with the other words and articles.

3.2

LEVEL
Intermediate+

FOCUS
Reading for gist, giving and listening to oral summaries, matching texts and titles

MATERIALS
Class set of a text

MATCHING THE TITLE TO THE STORY

This activity asks students to write their own headlines for articles.

SUGGESTED TEXTS
Any text longer than three paragraphs. Some examples of headlines, particularly from the popular press.

Preparation

1 Cut the text into paragraphs.

Procedure

1 Circulate the example headlines and ask students to consider the kind of articles that might follow them.
2 Get students to practise headline style by writing headlines for the following scenarios:

A boy jumps into a river to rescue his dog. His father jumps in to rescue the boy but does not succeed. The dog swims back alone.

A priest in Sussex agrees to marry homosexuals. His church has a long waiting list for marriages and conventional couples have to wait for months. The Bishop does not approve.

Cyndy James, the rock star, is divorcing her husband after a marriage which lasted only twenty four hours. She is alleging mental cruelty.

A scientist, Dr Jane Rawlins, is accusing her husband, Professor Thomas, of taking the credit for a discovery that she made. Dr. Rawlins was working on a project directed by Thomas and the couple are still living together.

3 Divide the class into pairs and give each pair a paragraph of the text.
4 Each pair constructs a headline to fit their paragraph. They can be witty or cryptic if they wish. They must produce two copies. If the text is part of a novel they must treat it as a newspaper story. Even a technical extract will stand this treatment, for example:

The steam passes into the condenser where it becomes water. The water is then recirculated to the boiler where it is reheated.

Wonder Condenser Keeps Water Going Round!

5 Shuffle the headlines and paragraphs. Each student takes a paragraph they have not read and a headline they have not written.
6 Students form groups with as many students as there are different paragraphs.
7 Ask each student to read their headline out loud. Repeat until every student has heard every other headline in the group. Use this for pronunciation practice.
8 Ask one student to explain the content of their article to the group. The student who thinks they have the headline of this article says nothing. The rest of the group must identify the person with the appropriate headline.

HEADLINE OR TITLE EXPANSION

A way to stimulate interest in a text by getting students to try to predict the text from its title, then to compare their predictions with what is actually written. The activity is complicated or straightforward according to the relationship between the title and text. Newspaper articles are generally easier to do, but literary texts can make the activity more challenging.

Procedure

1 Write the title or headline of the text on the board.
2 Ask the students to think about what a text with such a title or headline is likely to contain. They can talk about this in pairs. One way to get them going is to suggest a word association exercise, as follows:

   One partner says a word from the title. The other says something that this suggests to them (they should think before they speak). The first partner then asks for an explanation of this association, as related to the whole title. For example, for the title 'The Guarantee of Peace' the discussion might be as follows:

Student 1   Guarantee.
Student 2   A new car.
Student 1   Explain please.
Student 2   A new car always has a guarantee.
Student 1   Does this guarantee peace?
Student 2   Peace in my mind.

   Demonstrate with a student so that they get the idea.
3 Select a pair of students to come to the front of the class. Take them aside and tell them that they will be the text and that they should act as if they have a very close knowledge of it, although they have not, in fact, seen it yet.
4 Get the class to ask the pair questions that reveal the text. The questions should be based on the title thus expanding the title and making it into an oral text. It is important that the answers should sound as if the pair answering are genuinely aware of the content of the text. Again, for the example title 'The Guarantee of Peace' the questions might be as follows:

Student 1   What is the guarantee of peace?
Student 2   It's a drug that makes you happy.
Student 1   Can I buy it?
Student 2   Not yet. They're making it now.
Student 1   Who makes it?
Student 2   A drug company.

If the questions are slow in coming or dry up quickly, seed them in the class by distributing bits of paper with question prompts on them. This is also a way of bringing in shy students. You will have to be

3.3

LEVEL
Lower
intermediate+

FOCUS
Asking and
answering
questions,
predicting a text
from its title,
comparing a
predicted text and
a real text

MATERIALS
Class set of any
text

quick and scribble out the prompt as the last question is being answered. You can also put the prompts on the board. For example, 'What guarantee of peace?', 'Who/make it?' etc.

5 The class takes notes and stops when they feel they have extracted all the information about the text that they can.

6 Ask students to use their notes to make an oral class summary.

7 Distribute the text for rapid silent reading.

8 Divide the class into pairs. Each pair has to produce a maximum of five statements highlighting differences between the predicted text and the real text, such as 'The guarantee of peace is not a drug, it's the state security office.'

NOTE

One way to do an oral class summary is as follows:

Tell the class that when you touch a student, they should start speaking about the text. As soon as you touch another, this student should try to come in and the other should stop talking. Try for switches in mid-sentence and make the last speaker repeat what came before if they get lost. This is a very good way to get students to listen to each other.

VARIATION

This variation examines the relationship between title and text more closely. At an advanced level it will work best with more literary texts that have a complicated relationship between title and text.

Select two students to read the text before the lesson begins. These will 'be' the text in class. Proceed as in the above activity, except that the students answering the questions should reply with their real knowledge of the text. They should be careful not to give any more information about the text than is needed to answer each question.

Students decide how much the title reveals about the text and discuss the difference between what they were told about the text and the text itself.

3.4

LEVEL
Lower
intermediate+

FOCUS
Reading for gist,
discussing the
purpose of a text

MATERIALS
Class set of a text,
slips of paper

TRUE TITLE, FALSE TITLE

A quick activity based on the classic title-finding formula which encourages reading for gist and making a decision as to what a text is fundamentally about.

SUGGESTED TEXT

Literary or journalistic. Shorter texts are preferable. The following poem works well:

Originality?

He who must do
Something altogether new
Let him swallow his own head.

Chinweizu, *Voices from Twentieth Century Africa*, Faber and Faber 1988, p.238

Preparation

1 Separate the text from its title or headline and prepare one copy for each student in the class.
2 Prepare slips of paper large enough to write a title or headline on. Have one for each student.

Procedure

1 Give each student a slip of paper and a copy of the text without the title or headline.
2 Ask students to read the text and to write a suitable title on their slip of paper.
3 Deal individually with as many students as you can during the title writing stage and perfect the English of their title, even to the point of inserting idiom. When you are correcting, dictate the true title to one student and make sure that the rest of the class do not know that you are doing this. Tell the student privately that they will present this true title as their own.
4 Divide the class into two or more juries. Each jury should be a good-sized discussion group.
5 Each jury discusses all of the titles in order to find the best one.
6 Each jury presents its findings to the class and justifies them if their decisions are challenged.
7 The real title is revealed and the article is read again.

TRUE TEXT, FALSE TEXT

An activity based on distinguishing real from imagined texts which puts both the language and content of a text into play.

SUGGESTED TEXTS

One or more of any type. The number of texts depends on their length and how often you plan to repeat the activity in one class.

Preparation

Photocopy a class set of the text you have chosen. Also photocopy a text that resembles it physically, that is, a text which looks similar because it has a similar layout or design, but has a different content.

Procedure

1 Divide the class into pairs. Select a pair of students and give one of them a copy of the first text and the second a copy of the second text.
2 Write the title of the text on the board.
3 Ask the class to discuss possible texts that fit the title. Take the two students with texts outside. Tell them that the one with the text that fits the title must read it and that the other must only pretend to read

3.5

LEVEL
Intermediate+

FOCUS
Reading for gist, inventing titles, making oral summaries, asking and answering questions

MATERIALS
Class sets of texts

theirs. Say that the one who is pretending must build up an imaginary text that fits the title on the board. Help the one with the decoy text to get the idea by asking the kind of questions they may encounter in class. If the text was titled 'Mooncity', they may be asked 'Where is Mooncity?' 'Who goes there?' 'Who do they meet?' 'What do they do?' etc. It is important that this student does not know the content of the 'real' text.

4 The partner with the decoy text describes it to the class then the partner with the real text describes theirs to the class.

5 Tell the class one of the texts is imaginary. Encourage the class to ask questions to try to find out which text is real and which was imagined. Tell them to look for a consistent story line and also for psychological hints as to who is lying and who is telling the truth. They cannot ask students to read directly from the page. Get the class going by asking questions yourself.

6 Ask the class who they think has the real text and who has the decoy one. When they reach a consensus, they stop asking questions. Hand out copies of the first text. The students read the text in order to find out whether they were right or not.

3.6

GUIDED PREDICTIONS

LEVEL
Intermediate+

An activity to stimulate interest in a text and encourage understanding by using an information gap technique.

FOCUS
Expanding phrases, predicting a text, constructing oral or written summaries

SUGGESTED TEXT
Any titled text. The poem on page 83 can work at levels intermediate and above.

Procedure

MATERIALS
Class set of a text

1 Write the title of the text on the board.

2 Divide the class into two groups – a writing group and a reading group.

3 The writing group expand the title in the following way:
Each student takes a word from the title and writes a sentence explaining or elaborating upon it on a piece of paper. For example, for the title 'Hospital Visits', the sentence might be 'Hospitals make me sad'. Each student passes the paper to a neighbour who then writes another sentence elaborating on the one that has been written on the top of the paper, for example, 'We have to visit them'. The next student elaborates on the sentence that has just been written. This continues until each piece of paper has been passed round the group.

4 The reading group studies the text. They should read with dictionaries and make themselves familiar with its content. They can ask each other questions or do a contradiction exercise. (See Note below.)

Hospital Visits

At length to hospital
This man was limited,
Where screens leant on the wall
And idle headphones hung.
Since he would soon be dead
They let his wife come along
And pour out tea, each day.

I don't know what was said;
Just hospital-talk,
As the bed was a hospital bed.
Then one day she fell
Outside on the sad walk
And her wrist broke – curable
At Outpatients, naturally.

Thereafter night and day
She came both for the sight
Of his slowing-down body
And for her own attending,
And there by day and night
With her blithe bone mending
Watched him in decay.

Winter had nearly ended
When he died (the screen was for that).
To make sure her wrist mended
They had her in again
To finish a raffia mat –
This meant (since it was begun
Weeks back) he died again as she came away.

Philip Larkin, *Collected Poems*, Faber and Faber 1988 p73

5 A member of the writing group comes to the board and writes the first sentence from their list under the title.

6 A member of the reading group comes to the board and corrects or rewrites the sentence so that it reflects the content of the text. This is difficult as the student should try to keep the basic pattern of the sentence. You may need to intervene. Then a member of the writing group comes to the board and writes a sentence that expands the corrected one and the reading group change it again and so on. For example:

Old sentence	Hospitals make me sad.
Correction	The hospital is sad.
New expansion	We have to visit it.
Correction	An old woman has to visit it.

7 Continue until the activity exhausts itself or until most of the main points of the text are on the board.

NOTE

For a contradiction exercise:

A student makes a statement about the text that is either true or untrue. Another student agrees or disagrees and states what really happened. The students should try to trip each other up.

Student 1   The man was in hospital with a broken wrist.
Student 2   No, the woman broke her wrist when she went to see him.

3.7

LEVEL
Intermediate+

FOCUS
Reading for gist, writing rubrics, discussing the purpose of a text

MATERIALS
Class set of any text

RUBRIC WRITER

The rubric is really an expanded title. It gives possible readers a little bit more information so that they can decide whether to go ahead with the text or put it down. This is a simple activity that gives students a formula for writing rubrics and asks them to think clearly about the major points in a text.

Procedure

1 Give a copy of the text to each student.
2 Tell students to see the text as answering three questions. It may address only one big issue or many more. However every piece of writing can be seen as answering unasked questions and here students have to think of three. The poem 'Hospital Visits' (see page 83) might give:
   • Can a modern hospital give comfort to the dying?
   • What happens to the wife who visits her dying husband?
   • What is the real sadness of death in modern society?
3 Divide the students into pairs and ask them to read the text and decide which three big questions it answers.
4 When they have written down their three questions, ask students to tell you what they are. Write on the board the questions that are substantially different from each other and correct them as you do so.
5 If you have more than three questions on the board, tell the class that they must reduce the number to three. Get them to decide collectively which are the best three. Ask students to defend their own questions and say why they get at more of the text than others. If there is disagreement after discussion, put the matter to a vote. The most popular questions stay on the board.
6 Write on the board: 'These are the vital questions that the author tries to answer dealing with...'

7 Explain the meaning of the incomplete sentence. Ask the students to think in pairs of two separate topics in the text that relate to the questions on the board and would complete the sentence. For 'Hospital Visits' they might be:

- the state of mind of a hospital visitor.
- the drab circumstances of a death in modern England.

8 Write suggestions on the board and get the class to help you select the two topics they think work best. You may have to impose your opinion a little here.

9 Write on the board: 'In his/her fascinating poem/article/story/..'

10 Now get the students to put it all together to get the following type of rubric:

> Can a modern hospital give comfort to the dying? What happens to the wife who visits her dying husband? What is the real sadness of death in modern society? These are the vital questions that the author tries to answer in his fascinating poem, dealing with the state of mind of a hospital visitor and the drab circumstances of a death in modern England.

NOTE

If you have doubts about this for more specialised texts, a recent ESP training session produced the following amusing result for a text about plumbing systems:

> How do you keep the office warm? How do you give your employees water to wash? How do you get rid of waste? These are the vital questions that the author tries to answer in her fascinating article, dealing with pipes, drains, boilers and radiators.

CHAPTER 4

Affective texts

The activities in this book have dealt with the discourse and language of texts. By so doing they have tried to make the student more involved in even the most apparently inaccessible reading matter. In the following activities the search for greater student involvement becomes primary. The object is less to emphasise language and more to enhance its impact. The hope is that your classes will feel more inspired by the prospect of studying texts. This is not to say that the issues of word and sentence meaning or of discourse are simply cast aside or left to some process of automatic learning. I think that all learning demands effort in some sense and the object here is to make that effort more personally worthwhile. In some of these activities, the student is asked to distort an original meaning towards one that the writer never intended, yet this process, above all, may require a very close understanding of what that original meaning was.

4.1

LEVEL
Elementary+

FOCUS
Imagining a text, asking and answering questions

MATERIALS
Class set of two texts

INVISIBLE TEXTS

This is an inverted reading comprehension where only the questioner knows the text and where the answerer must invent their own. The activity therefore has two aims – an understanding of text by the questioner and the invention and description of an alternative by the answerer.

SUGGESTED TEXTS
Any two texts, which can be quite different, but it is useful if they are related in some way. They may be by the same author or originate from the same country, etc.

Procedure

1 Divide the class into two groups.
2 Give each member of each group a different text.
3 In their groups, the students divide into pairs.
4 Each pair reads the text and constructs a set of questions which will together reveal a complete understanding of the text. Students must understand that they are not writing questions about single words or points of grammar. They are writing an ordered list of questions that when answered would almost produce a summary of the text. Each student keeps a copy of the list of questions.
5 Each student finds a partner from the other group.

6 The students imagine they have read their partner's text.

7 Students who were in Group 1 ask their questions to students in Group 2. Students in Group 2 try to answer as consistently as if they had read the text, deducing what it was about from the questions they are asked. Students in Group 1 write the answers as they are given them.

8 Repeat with students in Group 2 asking students in Group 1.

9 Students use their answers to write a short summary of the text as their partner has imagined it.

10 Students read each other's texts and each other's summaries, pointing out likenesses and differences.

WHAT I WANT TO READ

This is a useful starter for a Monday morning, particularly for the text-weary ESP class. It will challenge students and leave them with a good appreciation of how a text is constructed. The text here is a frame inside which the student constructs something completely different.

SUGGESTED TEXTS
Any two texts that the students will not find too difficult.

Procedure

1 Ask the students to relax in any way they wish and to close their eyes. Ask them to imagine the place where they would most like to be at that moment. They imagine how it feels and how it looks. They imagine its scents and its sounds.

2 When the students are tired of their picture, they turn to a neighbour and discuss what they saw.

3 The students relax again. This time they imagine what they would most like to read about. They write down the title of this imaginary text.

4 Give the students a copy of the text each and tell them to alter it so that it deals with the subject they want to read about. They must do this by altering as little of the text as possible. It might be useful to show them the following text before they begin, by way of an example:

Digital recordings

Digitally encoded music, recorded direct, offers the purest signal. The electronics that decode the series of pulses, which are turned eventually into sound waves, allow none of the spurious distortion signals that are associated with other analog types of recording.

4.2

LEVEL
Upper
intermediate+

FOCUS
Remodelling a text,
listening and
reading
comprehension

MATERIALS
Class sets of texts

The altered text might read:

The Man I want to Meet

His thoughts are encoded like music, recorded direct, and send me the purest signal. His brain decodes my series of messages which are turned eventually into dreams and allows none of the distortion of signals that are associated with other types of relationship.

5 Circulate and correct the new texts as they are being written and help students to say what they want within the formula of the original text.
6 Students read their texts to each other in groups of four.

4.3

LEVEL
Intermediate+

FOCUS
Understanding the main stages in a process, narrating in the present simple, explaining feelings and sensations

MATERIALS
Class set of texts

CHANGING THE PERSPECTIVE

This activity makes students think closely about the language of the text by altering third person narratives so that they are seen from the view of a first person.

SUGGESTED TEXT
Any description of procedures, processes and systems, scientific, technical or economic instructions.

Preparation

1 Identify what you think are the main stages in the process being described. For example, a text about the four stroke cycle would give you:

1 Induction
2 Compression
3 Combustion
4 Exhaust

Procedure

1 Tell students the number of stages in the process.
2 Students read the text to find out what the stages are. They can make a flow chart, like the one on page 89 to illustrate the process.
3 Ask students to imagine they are the thing which is being processed and to think about telling the story of what happens to them. You might say: 'You are a drop of petrol, what happens to you in this process?'
4 Students in pairs tell the story of what happens to them.
5 One student goes to the board and writes, other students collectively dictate the whole experience of the element in question.
6 The class discuss key differences between the use of language in their story and in the original text. Encourage them to look not just at the grammatical changes but also at any changes in register.

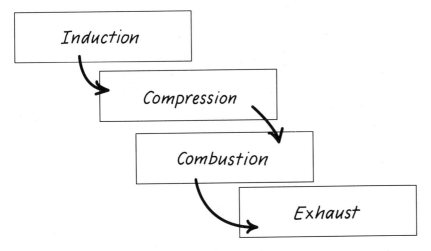

VARIATION

For third person narratives and descriptions. Students retell the story from the perspective of one of the characters. Students observe a scene from the view point of an object or particular character. They are careful to show how it affects them. This is often very rewarding when done from the view point of very minor characters, such as the good servant, who never says a word. Use your collective imagination – if minor characters are out of the scene put them back in or have them look through a key hole.

ACKNOWLEDGEMENT

This activity is indebted to an approach described in *English for Specific Purposes*, *A Learning-centred Approach* (Hutchinson and Walters 1987).

TEXT AS GUIDED FANTASY

I have often thought that the power of the word lies in the freedom that it affords its reader or listener. All writers try to make the reader understand what they understand and see what they see. But for me words allow more freedom than pictures. If the text says: 'I stopped by a river', the river can be any that the reader knows about or desires. If it were a photograph, the reader could only visualise the river in the picture. Words do not so much trap thoughts as guide them in a particular direction. All text is therefore a kind of guided fantasy and this activity is a straightforward exploitation of that view.

SUGGESTED TEXT

A literary text, poems, narratives or descriptions.

4.4

LEVEL
Intermediate+

FOCUS
Listening to a reading, discussing fantasies

MATERIALS
Class set of a text

Preparation

1 Preteach any difficult vocabulary in the text and deal with any other problem areas with the class at least the day before you do this activity. You can do this in a peer teaching session where students must first consult each other over the difficulties and only call on you as a last resort. The students must not see the text at this point.
2 Make a short list, for yourself, of some words or phrases that you think particularly important to the theme of the text.

Procedure

1 Try to make the class feel as relaxed as possible. They should settle in a way they find comfortable, put their heads down on desks or even lie on the floor and close their eyes. You can also lead them through a step-by-step relaxation exercise. If possible, play music which you think matches the tone of the text.
2 Tell the class that you want them to visualise, in as much detail as possible, everything in the text.
3 Read the text in a clear and unhurried manner. Your approach should be neither very expressive and dramatic nor too smooth and monotonous. The students just listen. Pause often so that they have time to picture what they hear.
4 If you have music, keep it playing after you have finished. Ask students to recount their experience of the text to each other in pairs or in small groups.
5 When the students have finished, ask one of them if there is any part of the text they particularly remember. Encourage them to say why this was so. Put the question to the class and ask them if they reacted in the same way.
6 Write on the board some of the words from the text that you thought were important. Ask the class to try to put the words in the context which the text led them to imagine, thinking also about their own associations and describing those thoughts to each other.
7 Hand out copies of the text. Students read it to themselves. Afterwards, ask them if there is any way in which their impressions of the text now differ from those they got when listening.

NOTE

Some students might say that they saw nothing when asked to visualise the text and that they do not fantasise. In this case, take any object from the text and ask one such student to describe it. The object could be something that is unimportant and undescribed. For example in the sentence: 'She walked up to the house and opened the door', the conversation might be as follows:

Teacher	Describe a door.
Student 1	A door!?
Teacher	Yes, describe a door. What's it made of?
Student 1	Wood, of course.

Teacher   What kind of wood? Hard wood?
Student 1 Yes, hard wood.
Teacher   And the colour? etc.

Insist that the student tell you everything about that door again, then point out that they have imagined that object. Ask them to think about other things in the text in a similar way.

VARIATION

Another approach is to write your own personalised account of some technical or scientific description. You could use the method suggested in Activity 4.3, *Changing the perspective* but using the second rather than the first person. You could say, for example, 'You are a petroleum molecule'. The activity will of course be more humorous and less intense in this case but it is an unusual way to deal with a dry text.

TEXT CHOICE, TEXT TRIBES

This is a useful way of introducing or finishing a study of the work of one writer or of discovering the interests of a class, though the variation can have a more general application. The activity demands that students should be ready to stretch their understanding to see a text as meaning something quite different from what the writer intended. However this cannot be done without a genuine grasp of what the text is really about.

SUGGESTED TEXTS

A selection of different texts. They can either be by the same or different writers. They might be different treatments of the same subject or about completely different things.

Preparation

Give copies of all the texts to each student and ask them to go away and read them.

Procedure

1 If the students have not read, or at least skimmed, all the texts, give them time to do so and sort out any comprehension problems.
2 Let the students decide which text they like best. Ask them to think first about language. Ask:
   ● Are there any particular words or phrases that you find powerful or unusual?
   ● Do you particularly like the writer's way of writing?
   Suggest they think about content second. Ask:
   ● Do you particularly enjoy the subject matter of the text?
   ● Is this because it is about something that has always interested you or because it is teaching you something new?

4.5

LEVEL
Intermediate+

FOCUS
Reading for a basic impression, expressing likes and dislikes, describing interests

MATERIALS
Class sets of texts

3 Ask the students to look for people in the class who like the same text as they do. They should form groups and discuss their common ground. Suggest they begin by answering the kinds of question you asked in Step 2. If students cannot find anybody with the same likes as them, then they must compromise and look for someone whose first choice is their second. If the whole class has the same first choice then tell some that they must look for a second or a third choice as you will need more than one group.

4 Explain that each group is a tribe for whom the text is their most sacred document. The text contains all they most care about. It expresses their common culture, albeit in a coded form. (With imagination, any text can be made to justify anything!) Tell each group to invent their culture and try to justify it with the text (or sub-text). If they get stuck, help them by showing how even the most arid text can be made to mean something else.

Allow no more than twenty minutes for this stage as students can get very involved. If the pace flags, move quickly to Step 5.

5 One tribe explains their text and culture to the rest of the class. Another tribe follows but they will also justify their own way of life by attacking the one they have just heard. They should object to even small cultural differences. Continue until every group has explained itself.

EXTENSION

If there are more than two tribes in the class, they can negotiate alliances with each other on the basis of their having similar outlooks. They justify their alliances by defending each other's text and the way of life it expresses. They can say why their allies' way of life is better than their opponents'.

VARIATION

A much more straightforward version of this activity is to divide the class into two groups and tell each group that they are a tribe and must write down their ten commandments – the ten basic rules by which they have decided to live. Each group is then given the same text and must interpret it as a sacred document which describes and justifies their way of life.

CHANGES OF TREATMENT

A rewarding activity which is best for sophisticated students, and demands a learning environment where a substantial cross-section of the English language press will be available to you. It also needs a major event that is likely to be covered by all of the papers.

SUGGESTED TEXTS
A series of newspaper articles on the same subject, from as many different kinds of newspaper as possible. If possible, one copy per student of each article.

Preparation

1 Try to find as many different articles on the same event as possible.
2 Distribute the articles for reading.

Procedure

1 Give one article to each student.
2 Students form groups with those who have the same article.
3 Each group works independently of the others and profiles a typical reader of their article; imagining his or her lifestyle, political views, occupation, age, frustrations, anxieties, income, aspirations, etc. They justify the profile with the article. Draw this information out with questions as you circulate.
4 Redistribute the articles so that each group has a new article.
5 End the group phase and call the class together, although the different group members should still sit near each other. Ask one member of each group to take on the character of the typical reader they have just profiled. The rest of the class interrogates them about their life and beliefs. They cannot refer to the content of the article.
6 The group who think they have the article of this typical reader should say so and justify their claim.
7 Continue until each group has profiled a typical reader and had the reader matched with an article.
8 Discuss differences in the treatment of the subject from a linguistic and philosophical point of view. Discuss the match between language and outlook.

4.6

LEVEL
Upper
intermediate+

FOCUS
Silent reading,
stylistic analysis,
describing people,
role play

MATERIALS
Newspaper articles

4.7

LEVEL
Lower
Intermediate+

FOCUS
Discussion, making
character studies,
asking questions

MATERIALS
Letters from
newspapers or
magazines

REVEALED LETTER WRITERS

The emphasis here turns from reader to writer and the activity includes a demanding stage where students plead for the possession of a particular text. Involving students in a text can make the second stage more interesting since the imagining of an unknown writer is easier to achieve after a close identification of reader and text.

SUGGESTED TEXTS

A selection of letters from the correspondence columns of newspapers or magazines, or other short texts that are clear expressions of opinion. They should be directly or indirectly revealing of the character or the attitudes of the writer. Letters from an agony column can also be used. One letter for every four or five students in the class. Enough copies of each letter for all students to have one text at the same time.

Preparation

Give each letter a number.

Procedure

1 Give every student a letter. Allow one minute for them to skim it then shout 'change'. All students then exchange letters and skim a new one.
2 Repeat until every student has skimmed every letter.
3 Put the letters in a pile in the centre of a table.
4 Appoint a student who you consider fair-minded to be the judge. Tell the judge to select any letters they like and to put them aside.
5 Take the judge aside and tell them they are going to listen to each student in turn say why they want a particular letter given back to them. Tell the judge that they will do nothing more than nod wisely and pretend to take notes. Only if the student's case dries up will they prompt with questions like: 'Can you continue?' and 'Is that all you have to say?'
6 Tell the class that they must decide which letter they want most and why. Not all the students will get the letters they want because there are not enough copies. Each in turn must then make a one-minute speech to the judge saying why they want the letter. Tell them it is very important they get the letter they want and that they must make a good case for it.
7 Ask the judge to hear every speech in turn and stress that their decision on who gets which letter will be based on the quality of the speeches.
8 After every case has been heard, ask the judge to say: 'I am sorry, your speeches were all too good. I cannot make any decision'. The judge then deals out the letters in a random order until every student, including themselves, has got one text.
9 Students with the same letter form groups. The judge is no longer needed and can return to the ranks of the students. In their groups students profile their letter writer, imagining their lifestyle, political

views, occupation, age, frustrations, anxieties, income, aspirations, etc. They imagine the kind of environment in which the letter writer lives, what the inside of their house looks like, the kinds of clothes they wear, etc.

10 The students think of questions which will best elicit information about their letter writer.

11 A student from one group comes to the front of the class to play the part of their letter writer while the others question them to find out who they are and what their views are.

12 Distribute the letter in question and discuss the appropriateness of the profile.

13 Repeat the activity with the other groups.

MY QUESTIONS

Many teachers realise that the laborious writing out of comprehension questions before a 'text class' can be a complete waste of time. As with so much preparation, it is better to get students to do it themselves. This is because question writing can demand as close a reading of a text as question answering.

Preparation

Divide the text into two roughly equal parts. Each part should make reasonable sense. Do not cut the text across a sentence.

Procedure

1 Divide the class into two groups. Give one half of the text to Group 1 and the other half to Group 2.

2 Write the following headings across the top of the board:

Ask the students to divide a piece of paper into four columns with these headings.

4.8

LEVEL
Elementary+

FOCUS
Stating areas of interest, asking and answering questions

MATERIALS
Class set of a text, bi- or monolingual dictionaries

3 Ask the students to read the text individually, using a dictionary, and to find things in it which they can write in these columns. Explain that 'Things I didn't know' is for any new knowledge that the text gives them. For some fiction this might arguably be everything since an entire world may have been invented. Students will therefore have to exercise judgement about what makes the most impact. 'Words I didn't know' and 'Things I couldn't say' refer to new vocabulary and unfamiliar forms of expression. If the text were artistic then 'Things I couldn't say' might refer to a use of language that makes a particularly strong impact.

People often read to have their own opinions confirmed. They feel more secure when someone else states their own opinions and perhaps argues their case more coherently. 'Things I wanted said' is for these kinds of points. It is also for those points the students have thought of before and particularly agree with. Again students should write down only what stands out most.

Students should also understand that they can leave some of these columns empty. However, if they were able to leave all of them empty, then I would suggest that they have been given the wrong text and that their time has been wasted.

Finally, it is sometimes hard to know what to put in which column. A point that the student particularly agrees with might also be said in a new way for them. There is no need to agonise about this. They simply put it in whatever column they feel like.

4 When the students have completed their part of the text and filled in the columns, ask them to form questions about some of the things they have written down. These questions should be formulated as pretext questions, or questions which the student reads the text to answer. The type of question should change according to the column where the information has been entered. 'Things I didn't know' and 'Things I wanted said' questions should be very straightforward: 'Read the text to find out why/how/who or when?' For example:

Find out why John killed his sister.
Find out about the uses of carbon fibre.
Find out the writer's opinion about the future of the Zulus in South Africa.

'Words I didn't know' could be written as two-way multiple choice questions:

In the text, 'depressed' is
a pushed down
b feeling unhappy

'Things I couldn't say' could also be this kind of multiple choice:

In the text, 'he revelled in hatred' means
a he took pleasure in hating
b he felt forced to hate

Or in a literary text it might be an annoying practical criticism type question:

What does the phrase 'a summer's day' tell you about the poet's feelings for his mistress?

Expect simple questions from elementary students and give students a lot of help with phrasing.

5 When every student has produced a good set of questions ask Group 1 to swap questions and text with Group 2. They should then read this unseen part of the text in order to answer the questions they have been given.

MIMING IT

The classic mime technique for eliciting text from students is given back to the class. In other words, it is the students who mime and elicit rather than you.

SUGGESTED TEXT
Any where the content can be mimed in some way.

Preparation

Cut the text so that you have one piece for every four or five students. Each piece should make complete sense. Do not cut through sentences.

Procedure

1 Divide the class into groups of four or five and give each a section of the text. It does not matter if some groups have the same section.
2 Ask each group to read their piece of text together, helping each other with any problems and calling on you as a last resort.
3 Tell each group to construct a mime which illustrates the main points in their section of text. Appoint one person in the group as writer. This person will not participate in the mime but will direct it.
4 Ask the group with the first section of text to begin their mime. They perform it once straight through, then they do it again in very short sections. At the end of each section the writer asks the class to tell them what this part of the mime is about, and writes down what is said in note form on the board. Remember that every student will have read part of the text so they will have more than just the mime to guide them.

4.9

LEVEL
Elementary+

FOCUS
Reading for detailed understanding, preparing and performing a mime

MATERIALS
Class set of a text

5 Repeat for each section of the text, leaving all the notes on the board.

6 In pairs, students use the notes on the board to write a summary of the whole text.

7 Distribute copies of the complete text. Students read it in order to give their own summaries a mark of A, B, C or D, for accuracy of content.

NOTE

Technical texts may seem impossible to mime. This is rarely so if students take a creative approach. It may be worth using the technique shown in Activity 4.3, *Changing the perspective* and make one of the students into a hero, such as a petrol molecule or whatever.

4.10

LEVEL
Intermediate+

FOCUS
Asking and answering questions, listening and note-taking, making group summaries

MATERIALS
Class set of a text

CONFUSED TEXTS

An activity that demands substantial preparation but rewards it hand-somely by generating discussion and argument.

Preparation

1 Make two versions of the text. One version should be a copy of the original. The other version should be close to the original but with some changes to its main ideas and to its detail. This will probably involve retyping, though it may be possible to just add a few key insertions and corrections to the original. The texts on pages 99 and 100 work well for intermediate students.

2 Take one of your stronger students aside and give them both versions of the text to go away and read. The rest of the class should not know that there are two versions of the text. This student should also know that he or she is going to talk about both versions of the text. It is also possible for you or another English speaker to take this role.

3 Divide the class into two roughly equal groups.

Procedure

1 Tell the student who has read the texts to go into a separate room or out into the corridor. Go with them and tell them that they are going to be asked questions about the text by each half of the class in turn. The first time they should answer using the first version of the text and the second time using the second version. On no account must anybody know that two versions of the text are being used.

2 Half of the class goes outside to interview the student about the first version of the text. They try to find out as much as they can without actually seeing the text, and make notes. Limit the time to about fifteen minutes per five hundred words.

In Court

Version 1

Mirtle turned towards the jury then back to the witness.

'So Miss Hamburger,' he said, 'you came out of the house on Friday morning at eight as usual.'

'Yes sir,' the witness almost whispered.

'You walked down the steps, is that right?'

'Yes.'

'Sound so uncertain,' muttered the judge, 'speak up, speak up.'

Miss Hamburger coughed. 'Yes sir,' she said more loudly.

'And you saw the assailant coming out of the newsagents opposite. Am I right?'

'Oh, you are sir,' she said with a strange gasp of admiration.

'And then?'

'Like I told you, he walked ten yards down the street...'

'Ten yards you say?'

'About that yes. Straight up to poor Mr. Crookshank. Took out a gun and shot him.'

'And what did you do?'

'Screamed, just screamed and screamed.'

'You didn't for instance walk back into the flat and close the door?'

'I just couldn't move, just couldn't move.' She squeezed a tear out of her left eye.

'You didn't notice a large red lorry parked in front of the newsagents.'

'Can't say I did.'

'The lorry was there, Miss Hamburger, just like on every other day.'

'Maybe it was.'

'It was.'

'And I suppose you have X ray vision Miss Hamburger. Because all this happened behind that red lorry.'

'X ray vision,' she laughed weakly, 'Yes, maybe I do, maybe I do.'

© Longman Group UK Ltd 1991

While Group 1 are outside try the following activity with Group 2.

i Write the title of the text on the board and any words or phrases that you think may cause comprehension problems in the order in which they appear in the text. Remember to use the second version of the text.

ii Either write up a definition of each problem word, or a sentence showing how it is used. Do not include the word itself in such sentences.

iii Ask students to try to match the word to its sentence or definition, then to look at the words and the title and to suggest what the text may be about. Do not give any indication yourself as to the text's subject matter.

In Court

Version 2

Mirtle turned towards the judge then back to the witness.
'So Miss Hamburger,' he said, 'you came out of the flat on Friday morning at eight as usual.'
'Yes sir,' the witness almost whispered.
'You waited for the lift, is that right?'
'Yes.'
'Sound so uncertain,' muttered the judge, 'speak up, speak up.'
Miss Hamburger coughed. 'Yes sir,' she said more loudly.
'And while you were waiting you looked out of the window and saw the assailant coming out of the supermarket opposite. Am I right?'
'Oh, you are sir,' she said with a little cry of terror.
'And then?'
'Like I told you, he walked ten yards down the street...'
'Ten yards you say?'
'About that yes. Straight up to poor Mr. Crookshank. Took out a knife and stabbed him.'
'And what did you do?'
'Screamed, and ran back to phone.'
'You didn't rush out to help the injured man?'
'I just couldn't move, just couldn't move.' She began to cry loudly.
'You didn't notice a large red lorry parked in front of the newsagents.'
'Yes, of course I did.'
'The lorry was there, Miss Hamburger, just like on every other day.'
'Yes, delivering something to the supermarket.'
'It was.'
'And of course, you were high up, so you could see over the lorry to where Mr. Crookshank stood.'
'I saw everything,' she asserted, round eyed, 'everything.'

© Longman Group UK Ltd 1991

3 When Group 1 comes back, tell Group 2 to go and interview the student outside. This time that student's answers will be about the second version of the text. Do not tell the group that they may have learnt about different versions of the same text.

4 Ask every member of Group 1 to pair off with a member from Group 2. Each pair must produce one summary of the text. Tell them that they should aim to get the content right and that they must not communicate with other pairs.

5 Let the students argue about the texts.

6 Settle any remaining disputes by giving everyone both versions to read.

INTERROGATED TEXTS

An activity that is built around a possible relationship between a piece of writing and a person. It asks students to form opinions about the value of a text and tries to get them to offer opinions about the 'what for and why' of a particular piece of reading matter, questions that cannot be answered without a sound understanding of the texts themselves.

Preparation

At the end of a previous lesson, hand out the texts and ask the class to go away and study them.

Procedure

1 Take back the texts that have been read outside the class.
2 Divide the class into groups of three or four. If there is more than one text, give different texts to different groups so that all texts will be studied again by an equal number of people.
3 The students study the text in groups as if it is a person who will have to justify its existence; i.e. its expenditure of vocabulary, its use of paper, its message, its manner of expression, etc.
4 Still seated in their groups the students imagine they are the text and conduct mini-interrogations of each other, justifying themselves in every way.
5 Select one group and say they are their text then appoint the rest of the class as 'Guardians of the Heaven for Texts'.
6 Inform the text that it is dead and asking for admission to the Heaven for Texts. It is outside the gate and must justify its existence in order to get in. If it says something like 'I don't know, ask my writer', more than twice, it will be sent to hell. The Guardians can interrogate it about every detail and facet of its existence. You should join the Guardians to get their questions going. They should be along these lines:
   - What was your purpose in life?
   - What are you trying to tell us about here?
   - Why did you use this word?
   - Listen to this sentence, what are you telling us here?
   - Look at this metaphor, are you trying to deceive us with beauty?
   - Well, what are you trying to do then?
   - Why are you made in such a boring way with all these numbered sentences?
   - What possible interest do you think the world could have in what you're telling them?

   Finally the Guardians may judge it a 'worthy' or 'unworthy text' and send it to heaven or hell.
7 Repeat with other texts or other groups of students if you wish.

4.11

LEVEL
Upper intermediate+

FOCUS
Studying a text to fully master its detail, asking and answering questions

MATERIALS
Class sets of any texts (one or more)

4.12

LEVEL
Elementary+

FOCUS
Analysing a text for
its form and
content, analysing
a teacher's motives
for presenting it

MATERIALS
Class set of a text

WHY ARE YOU DOING THIS TO US?

A simple and unusual way to approach a text which may also cause teachers to examine their own motives. It combines well with other activities. It can also be a way to get feedback about a course or of directing a new course towards class interests.

SUGGESTED TEXT
Any that the class do not know.

Preparation

Think deeply about why you are presenting this particular text to your class.

Procedure

1 Write the following categories on the board and check that they are understood:

Content/message
Vocabulary
Idiom
Grammar/structure
Function/notion

The last is optional and its inclusion should depend on whether it is already understood.

2 Ask the students to read the text individually and then to decide why you have given it to them. They should think about each of the separate categories and see if they can find reasons for each within the text.

3 The class should form groups of three or four. Each group should produce a set of reasons why you gave them the text.

4 Appoint a confident student to role play you.

5 The class interrogate this student about why they gave out this text.

6 When the role play has run out of momentum, you should tell the class about any other motives for giving the text that they have not discovered.

7 Get the class to tell you what they would really like to read about and why, or to congratulate you on your choice.

ESCAPED TEXT

Perhaps the chapter number will make you feel unlucky with this activity for a start. Then the apparent complexity of the instructions will put you off completely! However this is nothing like as difficult to set up as it may seem, particularly as many students will recognise this activity as a kind of computer game put back into the class. It is self-contained and is an excellent way to wean students away from talking round hand-outs and towards the invention of their own texts.

LEVEL
Intermediate+

FOCUS
Describing journeys and places, deciding where to go, narrating the past

SUGGESTED TEXT
You will need one copy of the set of cards on page 104 for each group of ten. Once you have played the game a few times, you can invent your own cards.

MATERIALS
Copies of Location and Key Cards

Preparation

1 Photocopy one set of the location cards on page 104 for each group. The groups should not be smaller than eight or larger than fourteen.
2 Make key cards as shown either by photocopying the card on page 104 or by drawing a key on to a piece of card. Provide one key card for every two students in the class.

Procedure

1 Divide the class into groups of about ten.
2 Divide each group equally into five 'travellers' and five 'locations'. If this is not possible, always have exactly five locations. If you have more than five travellers, the fifth and sixth must travel in a pair. Seven travellers would give you two pairs, etc.
3 Tell the travellers to discuss the idea of mysterious journeys and to brainstorm appropriate vocabulary while you take the other students outside.
4 Give each location student one of the location cards you have prepared.
5 Give the student with the second location as many key cards as there are travellers in the group.
6 Explain the following:
   Each student is a place that can describe itself.
   Each location has a number. The locations sit in numerical order.
   They have to describe the location on the card to whoever comes to them. At the bottom of every card there are two alternative destinations. After they have described themselves, the locations must ask the traveller which of these destinations they want to go to. They then send the traveller to that location. For example, a traveller comes to location 4:

Location 4   You are in the middle of a dark forest. In front of you the trees are too thick to pass through. Near you there is one tall tree which you could climb. Behind you there is a path going back into the wood. Where do you want to go now? Back down the path or up the tree?

Traveller   Back down the path.

Location 4   Go to student 2.

1

You are near the river.
The river snakes away to the south through a steep valley.
On the other side there is a castle.

2 To the castle.
3 To the South.

1

2

You are standing outside a castle .
It is old and uninhabited.
The gate is open a little and you see tall grass growing inside.
Behind you there is a river.

1 To the river.
KEY into the castle.

2

3

You are standing on the edge of a dark forest.
Behind you, a river winds back through a steep valley.

1 Back to the river.
4 Into the forest.

3

4

You are in the middle of a dark forest. In front of you the trees are too thick to pass through. Near you there is one tall tree which you could climb. Behind you there is a path going back into the wood.

3 Go back down the path.
5 Climb the tree.

4

5

You have climbed to the top of the tree. You can see across a forest to a range of mountains in the South. To the North you see trees and a river flowing through a steep valley. There is a castle on a hill. To the East and West there are only trees.

4 Go back down the tree.
5 Stay put.

5

KEY

KEY

© Longman Group UK Ltd. 1991

When a traveller comes to location 2 they have the choice – to the river or into the castle. If the traveller goes into the castle, location 2 gives them a key card.

When a traveller has a key card, location 2 can then send them anywhere and tell them to present the key. When a traveller presents a key, the location does not describe the place on its card. Instead it does as follows:

i Asks the traveller where they have been and where they have decided to go.

ii Invents a new location to fit the traveller's story.

iii Asks them where they want to go next.

iv Sends them to any available location and tells them to present their key.

Therefore travellers with keys leave the text and move from one invented location to another without at first knowing it. They thus travel through a story of the location students' collective imagination. These students should not be told that their decisions about where they go are having no effect on where they are sent to. For example:

Location 2   You are standing outside a castle. It is old and uninhabited. The gate is open a little and you see tall grass growing inside. Behind you there is a river. Where do you want to go? To the river or into the castle?

Traveller   Into the castle.

Location 2   (Sees that nobody is talking to location 4). Go to the fourth student, over there, and show this key (gives the traveller a key card).

The traveller goes to location 4 and presents the key.

Location 4   (sees the key.) Where have you just been?

Traveller   I saw a castle with tall grass inside and I went in.

Location 4   Ah yes. (Describing from their imagination) In front of you is a stone staircase. It is dark and narrow. Below you there is a dark hole and a rope. Where will you go?

Traveller   Down the rope.

Location 4   (Sees that nobody is talking to location 1.) OK. Go and show your key to the first student, there.

Traveller   (Presents key to the first student.)

Location 1   Where have you just come from?

Traveller   Into a castle where I got this key. Then down a rope into a hole.

Location 1   Into a hole? There is water under you. Do you go up or let go of the rope? etc.

7 The location students come back into the room, and sit in numerical order. You send a student to each location (as far as numbers allow) and the activity begins.

8 When the different travellers appear to be losing momentum bring the group together and ask the travellers to recount their adventures.

Bibliography

Austen, J 1967 *Pride and Prejudice* Pan Books

Chinweizu, I in 1988 *Voices from Twentieth Century Africa* Faber and Faber

Ford Madox Ford 1982 *Parade's End* Penguin

Hill, C 1988 *The World Turned Upside Down* Peregrine Books

Hutchinson, T and Walters, A 1987 *English for Specific Purposes, A Learning-centred Approach* CUP

Larkin, P 1988 *Collected Poems* Faber and Faber

Mayhew, H 1862, 1950 *London's Underworld* William Kimber and Co.

Morgan, J and Rinvolucri, M 1986 *Vocabulary* OUP

O'Barney, G 1981 *The Global 2000 Report to the President* Blue Angel Inc.

De Pietro, R 1988 *Strategic Interaction: Learning Languages through Scenarios* CUP

Shakespeare, W 1926 *Macbeth* in *The Complete Works of Shakespeare* OUP